The Essential Buyer's Guide
TRIUMPH
HERALD & VITESSE
All models 1959 to 1971

Your marque expert:
Iain Ayre

VELOCE PUBLISHING
THE PUBLISHER OF FINE AUTOMOTIVE BOOKS

More Essential Buyer's Guides ...

- Alfa Romeo Alfasud (Metcalfe)
- Alfa Romeo Alfetta: all saloon/sedan models 1972 to 1984 & coupé models 1974 to 1987 (Metcalfe)
- Alfa Romeo Giulia GT Coupé (Booker)
- Alfa Romeo Giulia Spider (Booker)
- Audi TT (Davies)
- Audi TT Mk2 2006 to 2014 (Durnan)
- Austin-Healey Big Healeys (Trummel)
- BMW Boxer Twins (Henshaw)
- BMW E30 3 Series 1981 to 1994 (Hosier)
- BMW GS (Henshaw)
- BMW X5 (Saunders)
- BMW Z3 Roadster (Fishwick)
- BMW Z4: E85 Roadster and E86 Coupé including M and Alpina 2003 to 2009 (Smitheram)
- BSA 350, 441 & 500 Singles (Henshaw)
- BSA 500 & 650 Twins (Henshaw)
- BSA Bantam (Henshaw)
- Choosing, Using & Maintaining Your Electric Bicycle (Henshaw)
- Citroën 2CV (Paxton)
- Citroën DS & ID (Heilig)
- Cobra Replicas (Ayre)
- Corvette C2 Sting Ray 1963-1967 (Falconer)
- Datsun 240Z 1969 to 1973 (Newlyn)
- DeLorean DMC-12 1981 to 1983 (Williams)
- Ducati Bevel Twins (Falloon)
- Ducati Desmodue Twins (Falloon)
- Ducati Desmoquattro Twins – 851, 888, 916, 996, 998, ST4 1988 to 2004 (Falloon)
- Fiat 500 & 600 (Bobbitt)
- Ford Capri (Paxton)
- Ford Escort Mk1 & Mk2 (Williamson)
- Ford Focus RS/ST 1st Generation (Williamson)
- Ford Model A – All Models 1927 to 1931 (Buckley)
- Ford Model T – All models 1909 to 1927 (Barker)
- Ford Mustang – First Generation 1964 to 1973 (Cook)
- Ford Mustang – Fifth Generation (2005-2014) (Cook)
- Ford RS Cosworth Sierra & Escort (Williamson)
- Harley-Davidson Big Twins (Henshaw)
- Hillman Imp (Morgan)
- Hinckley Triumph triples & fours 750, 900, 955, 1000, 1050, 1200 – 1991-2009 (Henshaw)
- Honda CBR FireBlade (Henshaw)
- Honda CBR600 Hurricane (Henshaw)
- Honda SOHC Fours 1969-1984 (Henshaw)
- Jaguar E-Type 3.8 & 4.2 litre (Crespin)
- Jaguar E-type V12 5.3 litre (Crespin)
- Jaguar Mark 1 & 2 (All models including Daimler 2.5-litre V8) 1955 to 1969 (Thorley)
- Jaguar New XK 2005-2014 (Thorley)
- Jaguar S-Type – 1999 to 2007 (Thorley)
- Jaguar X-Type – 2001 to 2009 (Thorley)
- Jaguar XJ-S (Crespin)
- Jaguar XJ6, XJ8 & XJR (Thorley)
- Jaguar XK 120, 140 & 150 (Thorley)
- Jaguar XK8 & XKR (1996-2005) (Thorley)
- Jaguar/Daimler XJ 1994-2003 (Crespin)
- Jaguar/Daimler XJ40 (Crespin)
- Jaguar/Daimler XJ6, XJ12 & Sovereign (Crespin)
- Kawasaki Z1 & Z900 (Orritt)
- Land Rover Discovery Series 1 (1989-1998) (Taylor)
- Land Rover Discovery Series 2 (1998-2004) (Taylor)
- Land Rover Series I, II & IIA (Thurman)
- Land Rover Series III (Thurman)
- Lotus Elan, S1 to Sprint and Plus 2 to Plus 2S 130/5 1962 to 1974 (Vale)
- Lotus Europa, S1, S2, Twin-cam & Special 1966 to 1975 (Vale)
- Lotus Seven replicas & Caterham 7: 1973-2013 (Hawkins)
- Mazda MX-5 Miata (Mk1 1989-97 & Mk2 98-2001) (Crook)
- Mazda RX-8 (Parish)
- Mercedes-Benz 190: all 190 models (W201 series) 1982 to 1993 (Parish)
- Mercedes-Benz 280-560SL & SLC (Bass)
- Mercedes-Benz G-Wagen (Greene)
- Mercedes-Benz Pagoda 230SL, 250SL & 280SL roadsters & coupés (Bass)
- Mercedes-Benz S-Class W126 Series (Zoporowski)
- Mercedes-Benz S-Class Second Generation W116 Series (Parish)
- Mercedes-Benz SL R129-series 1989 to 2001 (Parish)
- Mercedes-Benz SLK (Bass)
- Mercedes-Benz W123 (Parish)
- Mercedes-Benz W124 – All models 1984-1997 (Zoporowski)
- MG Midget & A-H Sprite (Horler)
- MG TD, TF & TF1500 (Jones)
- MGA 1955-1962 (Crosier)
- MGB & MGB GT (Williams)
- MGF & MG TF (Hawkins)
- Mini (Paxton)
- Morgan Plus 4 (Benfield)
- Morris Minor & 1000 (Newell)
- Moto Guzzi 2-valve big twins (Falloon)
- New Mini (Collins)
- Norton Commando (Henshaw)
- Peugeot 205 GTI (Blackburn)
- Piaggio Scooters – all modern two-stroke & four-stroke automatic models 1991 to 2016 (Willis)
- Porsche 356 (Johnson)
- Porsche 911 (964) (Streather)
- Porsche 911 (991) (Streather)
- Porsche 911 (993) (Streather)
- Porsche 911 (996) (Streather)
- Porsche 911 (997) – Model years 2004 to 2009 (Streather)
- Porsche 911 (997) – Second generation models 2009 to 2012 (Streather)
- Porsche 911 Carrera 3.2 (Streather)
- Porsche 911SC (Streather)
- Porsche 924 – All models 1976 to 1988 (Hodgkins)
- Porsche 928 (Hemmings)
- Porsche 930 Turbo & 911 (930) Turbo (Streather)
- Porsche 944 (Higgins)
- Porsche 981 Boxster & Cayman (Streather)
- Porsche 986 Boxster (Streather)
- Porsche 987 Boxster and Cayman 1st generation (2005-2009) (Streather)
- Porsche 987 Boxster and Cayman 2nd generation (2009-2012) (Streather)
- Range Rover – First Generation models 1970 to 1996 (Taylor)
- Range Rover – Second Generation 1994-2001 (Taylor)
- Range Rover – Third Generation L322 (2002-2012) (Taylor)
- Reliant Scimitar GTE (Payne)
- Rolls-Royce Silver Shadow & Bentley T-Series (Bobbitt)
- Rover 2000, 2200 & 3500 (Marrocco)
- Royal Enfield Bullet (Henshaw)
- Subaru Impreza (Hobbs)
- Sunbeam Alpine (Barker)
- Triumph 350 & 500 Twins (Henshaw)
- Triumph Bonneville (Henshaw)
- Triumph Herald & Vitesse (Ayre)
- Triumph Spitfire and GT6 (Ayre)
- Triumph Stag (Mort)
- Triumph Thunderbird, Trophy & Tiger (Henshaw)
- Triumph TR2 & TR3 - All models (including 3A & 3B) 1953 to 1962 (Conners)
- Triumph TR4/4A & TR5/250 - All models 1961 to 1968 (Child & Battyll)
- Triumph TR6 (Williams)
- Triumph TR7 & TR8 (Williams)
- Triumph Trident & BSA Rocket III (Rooke)
- TVR Chimaera and Griffith (Kitchen)
- TVR S-series (Kitchen)
- Velocette 350 & 500 Singles 1946 to 1970 (Henshaw)
- Vespa Scooters – Classic 2-stroke models 1960-2008 (Paxton)
- Volkswagen Bus (Copping)
- Volkswagen Transporter T4 (1990-2003) (Copping/Cservenka)
- VW Golf GTI (Copping)
- VW Beetle (Copping)
- Volvo 700/900 Series (Beavis)
- Volvo P1800/1800S, E & ES 1961 to 1973 (Murray)

WWW.VELOCE.CO.UK

First published in February 2020 by Veloce Publishing Limited, Veloce House, Parkway Farm Business Park, Middle Farm Way, Poundbury, Dorchester DT1 3AR, England.
Tel +44 (0)1305 260068 / Fax 01305 250479 / e-mail info@veloce.co.uk / web www.veloce.co.uk or www.velocebooks.com.
ISBN: 978-1-787115-19-4; UPC: 6-36847-01519-0.

© 2020 Iain Ayre and Veloce Publishing. All rights reserved. With the exception of quoting brief passages for the purpose of review, no part of this publication may be recorded, reproduced or transmitted by any means, including photocopying, without the written permission of Veloce Publishing Ltd. Throughout this book logos, model names and designations, etc, have been used for the purposes of identification, illustration and decoration. Such names are the property of the trademark holder as this is not an official publication. Readers with ideas for automotive books, or books on other transport or related hobby subjects, are invited to write to the editorial director of Veloce Publishing at the above address. British Library Cataloguing in Publication Data – A catalogue record for this book is available from the British Library. Typesetting, design and page make-up all by Veloce Publishing Ltd on Apple Mac. Printed and bound by CPI Group (UK) Ltd, Croydon, CR0 4YY.

Introduction
– the purpose of this book

I've written several thousand articles in assorted motoring magazines, and 17 motoring books, about everything from Amphicars to Zodiacs. I'm a regular contributor to the authoritative and entertaining *Triumph World* magazine, and count several full-blown Triumph obsessives among my friends.

I don't currently drive a Herald or a Vitesse, mainly because I've just rescued a rough TR6. It's the next class of drug you move on to after your Vitesse. After a great deal of hands-on experience – good and bad – of 1960s and 1970s Triumphs, I genuinely and strongly recommend that you buy a Herald or a Vitesse.

A Vitesse is a Triumph Herald with a bigger engine; it shares much of its mechanics, and, because there's a great deal of crossover with other, smaller Triumphs, such as Spitfire and GT6, parts availability and prices are excellent.

The Vitesse is to the Herald as the GT6 is to the Spitfire. It's a faster, heavier six-cylinder version, but it has the same bodywork apart from the four-headlamp bonnet, which, even so, fits the same mountings, and only really differs in the flip front bonnet panel.

The separate chassis of the Herald family is rather old-fashioned for a car designed in the late 1950s, but Standard Triumph had little choice in the matter – its body manufacturer, Fisher and Ludlow, had been bought by the competition, BMC, and it was much easier for Triumph to find sub-contract manufacturers for a smaller separate chassis and panels than to source a manufacturer of a full monocoque body. However, that separate chassis has allowed these cars to last longer than many of their contemporaries, and makes them easier to restore, repair and service. The engine was a safe choice, based on the proven overhead valve 848cc Standard 10 unit.

A big range of transformational bolt-on body options for the small-Triumph family was a bonus, with Heralds appearing as saloons, estate cars, convertibles, coupés, and vans on the same chassis. In 1962 the Herald morphed into a sports car called the Spitfire, with more or less the same structure but a shorter chassis, and using the body sills and underfloor outriggers as structural members.

The chassis may have been old-fashioned, but the styling was at the cutting edge, and showed the way out

Triumph World magazine has celebrated classic Triumphs for decades and is very useful indeed, with classified ads as well as tech and resto stories.
www.triumph-world.co.uk

of the dull 1950s. Giovanni Michelotti designed the Triumph range, bringing sharp, light, Italian style to a country and time where most cars looked like plum puddings with portholes.

Heralds, and even Vitesses, are not high-performance cars, and they don't handle particularly well. The centre of gravity is low and the front suspension is very good, but there isn't really much power, and the transverse single spring geometry of the rear suspension of most older Triumphs is suspect,

The Spitfire chassis in the foreground differs from the Herald chassis behind only in being 8in shorter and having no rear outriggers. The mechanicals are virtually interchangeable.

although useful improvements were made later in the Vitesse's production life. The 1967 MkII Vitesse got revised rear suspension with new lower wishbones, Rotoflex driveshaft couplings, and rear camber changes controlled, but Heralds did not.

The bonnet changed for the 13/60, but from 1959 to the last of the 12/50s in 1967, the old-fashioned rounded wings ruled.

The main body structure on this 1959 Herald 948 stayed the same until the end of production.

Launch price in 1959 was ●x700, compared to the Mini at ●x500, and the Ford Anglia at ●x600. In the end, Minis and their stablemate 1100 variants sold two million each and Cortinas sold one million. Heralds sold 521,000 and Vitesses 51,000. The Triumph 1300 was supposed to replace the Herald family from 1965, but failed, selling only 113,000.

Heralds are still quite cheap to buy; they are light to drive and light on the pocket. The mechanics are simple and generally reliable, and spares are freely and cheaply available. A bonus with both Heralds and Vitesses is the avoidance of having to grovel under the car or lean over the front wings while dealing with the engine and front suspension: the huge flip front means you can sit on a wheel while working on the engine.

With the roof down, the side windows wound up, and the heater on, you can enjoy a convertible Herald or Vitesse all year round. Sunny winter mornings will tempt you out for a roof-down drive, and you should just yield and enjoy it.

948cc engine isn't what you might call a fireball, but it is very economical.

The early cars had a dashboard made of the same cheap paper-ish fibre stuff as the gearbox cover, (also used to make egg boxes and Trabants). Not nice, not strong, not attractive.

The convertible Heralds are more entertaining than the saloons, but just as practical. Try out both to see which flavour you like.

The Vitesse essentially adds two cylinders and some trim and mechanical upgrades, but it completely transforms the feel of the car.

The Vitesse is quite a different animal from a Herald, although sharing a high percentage of its shell, chassis and mechanical parts. It's a fine home for the 1600cc and the 2-litre straight-six. Vitesses do not balance particularly well, as the extra weight of the additional two cylinders on the cast iron block and head is too far forward, and the few hardcore Triumphisti who race Vitesses tend to shift the engine back a foot or so to stop them understeering and ploughing straight on into the kitty litter.

Having said that, they're fine for road use and I never thought of my Vitesses as handling badly while using them as daily drivers.

If it becomes a trend that Herald values rise faster than Vitesse values, I would definitely go for a Vitesse, as its fun-per-quid ratio is higher than that of a Herald.

Timeline
1959 – 948 Saloon and Coupé launched
1960 – 948 Convertible launched
1961 – 1200 and Estate launched
1962 – Van and Vitesse MkI launched
1963 – 12/50 sunroof Saloon launched. Heralds get stronger Vitesse chassis and disc brakes
1964 – Coupé deleted
1966 – Vitesse 2-litre launched
1967 – 13/60 launched, Vitesse becomes MkII, improved suspension
1970 – Saloon production ends
1971 – Convertible, Estate and Vitesse production ends

Herald coupé is an increasingly rare variant, but other than its rarity it's just a slightly less useful Herald.

The author's Vitesse in the 1980s: it wasn't a classic then, just a nice old car. I'm wishing now that I'd kept it.

The Essential Buyer's Guide™ currency
At the time of publication a BG unit of currency "●" equals approximately £1.00/US$1.32/Euro 1.18. Please adjust to suit current exchange rates.

Contents

Introduction
– the purpose of this book 3

1 Is it the right car for you?
– marriage guidance 9

2 Cost considerations
– affordable, or a money pit? 16

3 Living with a Herald or Vitesse
– will you get along together? 20

4 Relative values
– which model for you? 27

5 Before you view
– be well informed 33

6 Inspection equipment
– these items will really help 38

7 Fifteen minute evaluation
– walk away or stay? 41

8 Key points
– where to look for problems 45

9 Serious evaluation
– 60 minutes for years of enjoyment 48

10 Auctions
– sold! Another way to buy your dream 64

11 Paperwork
– correct documentation is essential! 69

12 What's it worth?
– let your head rule your heart 72

13 Do you really want to restore?
– it'll take longer and cost more than you think 75

14 Paint problems
– bad complexion, including dimples, pimples and bubbles 80

15 Problems due to lack of use
– just like their owners, Triumphs need exercise! 83

16 The Community
– key people, organisations and companies in the Triumph world 85

17 Vital statistics
– essential data at your fingertips 88

Index 94

Notes 95

1 Is it the right car for you?
– marriage guidance

A really good Vitesse is a pleasure to drive – light and responsive.
(Courtesy Paul Barlow)

It would be an unusual petrolhead or aesthete who didn't like a Herald or a Vitesse. Designer Giovanni Michelotti was a talented automotive sculptor, and his Triumphs have very good proportions. They are enjoyable and easy to drive within their performance limits, and they are among the cheapest and easiest classics to own.

The Vitesse in particular is a very attractive package, and, even if you're set on a Herald, I would recommend checking out a Vitesse: the smooth power and the absolutely delicious exhaust soundtrack really are something special, and, to my mind, are worth the extra buying price and lower fuel economy – although it's still 25mpg+ per Imperial gallon.

I'm about to get started on a TR6 project bought for a price that it would have been rude to refuse, and a critically important reason for getting involved in all the upcoming welding and kak is the sound and the silky grunt of an inadequately silenced Triumph straight-six.

Tall & short drivers
Even fairly large people can fit comfortably into a Herald or Vitesse. The seats go quite far back, and there's good height in the cockpit when the roof's up. Depending on location, weather and length of journey, the roof on the convertible models can also be folded back for unlimited headroom.

Weight of controls
Triumph steering is always pleasantly light, and the Herald was designed as a family car to be driven by all, so there are no macho pedal pressures. There's usually no

9

Early 948cc saloon is a pleasant and usable car: values of the early examples may go up, as early Minis are doing.

servo, so the brakes require a manual level of foot pressure, which may be unfamiliar to modern-car drivers – but you would forget that within a mile. I did once buy a Vitesse with a brake servo, but it locked up the front wheels far too easily so I deleted it.

The extra weight of the cast iron straight-six inevitably adds some weight to the front of the Vitesse, but thinking back, I cannot remember ever noticing any extra steering wheel weight when owning or driving them, whereas I actively dislike the heavy steering of a standard MGB. The Triumph steering is sensitive as well as light, and the turning circle is absurdly tight: you can U-turn in most side-roads, but it's not particularly good for the trunnions or the tyres.

Coupé variant is rare and could be a good investment, but has slightly ungainly proportions.

Will it fit in the garage?

Not only will a Herald or Vitesse fit in a garage, it will easily fit in a standard tiny 1930s British suburban garage. Length is 153in (3886mm) and width is 60in (1524mm). For comparison, a real Mini measures 120in x 55in, and a two-door BMW 'Mini' measures 150in x 68in, so a Herald is smaller than a new two-door BMW 'Mini' but a couple of feet longer than a real Mini.

The doors are also small enough to be opened in cramped garages,

Interior space

Better than many contemporaries. The dashboard is not too close, and the very slim pillars and big windows mean there is a great feeling of light and space. The seats are small and skinny with little padding and with no headrests, which means a little more room.

Luggage capacity

The Herald/Vitesse boot is of a reasonable size at approximately 13 cubic feet, and the back seat folds down for great flexibility. The Estate offers immense practicality if you need that. A full-size spare wheel occupies some of the boot, and filling that with tools and spares is the traditional approach, but relocating the spare to a boot rack for longer trips offers much increased luggage space. The back seats offer further luggage capacity, although there's no security as far as prying eyes goes.

You can't go wrong with a convertible car in a temperate climate. Even frosty February runs are fun.

The 13/60 flip front was modernised, using the same attractive bonnet shape as the Vitesse, but with single rather than dual headlights.

Running costs

I'm not sure that motoring gets much cheaper than a well-maintained Herald. A 1300 should regularly achieve well over 30mpg Imperial. A Vitesse will be in the mid to high twenties, driven sensibly. Tuning, correct tyre pressures and cruising the empty left lane on UK motorways will facilitate even better mpg.

Insurance is very cheap for classic cars in the UK, as classic car owners generally look after their carefully chosen pride and joy. They're also not morons and don't generally do stupid stuff like texting and driving, or drink-driving.

This was a successful update, upgrading the car to sharp Sixties modernity. The back, in this case an estate, remained the same.

Other running costs are based on these cars being used for hobby purposes and repaired at hobby prices, rather than blackmail commercial mainstream prices based on people needing their car to get to work – so while a headlight for a BMW 'Mini' might be a thousand pounds, a sealed-beam headlight for a Herald is 🟡x15. A coil pack for a Mazda MX5 is 🟡x300 or so, but Triumphs don't have a quadruple coil pack, they just have one coil. Those have suffered brutal price inflation recently and now also retail for around 🟡x15.

A 1950s-designed Triumph engine will not, however, survive hundreds of thousands of hard miles like a Mazda engine, without rebuilds. 70,000 or 80,000 miles would be a good life for a Triumph engine, although the straight-six in particular will rattle and smoke on far beyond that. One 2500cc TR5 straight-six engine of my acquaintance has covered 400,000 miles of US highway driving, with religiously observed oil changes and regular hard exercise.

MOT tests are no longer required for cars more than 40 years old, which now includes most Heralds. However, this was a stupid idea unless it's part of a longer-term plan to get old cars off the road. We very strongly recommend that you continue with an annual MOT, not least because the results of neglect compound year on year. I don't face an annual MOT test in Canada, so my Mini deteriorated to scrap rather than having to be annually repaired. It's human nature to postpone work, so pretend the annual MOT is still compulsory. Do it in the spring when the car comes out to play.

Usability

Nearly all car journeys in the UK involve one person driving just a few miles. In which case, a Herald is exactly as usable as any other car. Perhaps more so, as you can flip the roof back on the convertible and sunroof versions to carry a Christmas tree or a cello: the lovely big folding Webasto fabric sunroof is standard on the 12/50. There's enough room for substantial shopping.

A carburettor or carburettors and a contact-point ignition setup is inherently less reliable than modern kit, but can usually be fettled into getting you home using a nail file or the spares you carry in a bag inside the spare wheel, while any electric or electronic failure in a newer car sees it going on a flatdeck to a main dealer.

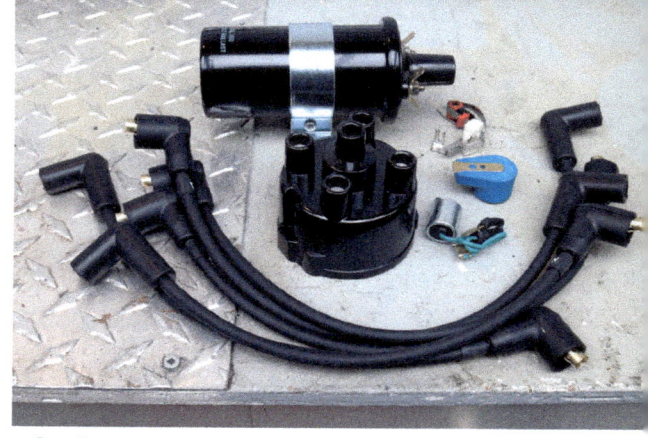

Service parts are very cheap; sometimes just a small percetage of the parts costs for a modern car. A Herald is far cheaper to buy and run than a new car.

One downside is vulnerability in an accident. In a major crash, a smaller Triumph tends to disintegrate, and there is no real side protection at all. For a car in regular city use, fitting a substantial roll over bar with backward and forward bars would be worth thinking about.

Parts availability

Halfords no longer carries much in the way of parts for older cars, although it's excellent if you need a bicycle or a universal car floor mat. The very competitive Triumph parts supply industry, however, will despatch pretty well anything you might need for a classic Triumph the same day by courier or post.

They all advertise in *Triumph World*, but the majors include TD Fitchett, Rimmer Brothers, and Moss.

The later 1300cc engine in the 13/60 has a lot more go than the 948 and the 1200.

13

Of course the best way to get parts at the right price is to join the Triumph Sports Six Club and track down fellow members close to you. All Triumph bunnies have a stash of spares in their garages and they will happily help you out with good secondhand stuff, which is often traded in a currency of returned help, beer and tea.

Parts costs
Thinking back to my last Triumph and its needs yields some sample current parts costs –
   Trackrod ends ●x9.50 each
   Door skin ●x85
   Fibreglass gearbox cover x●37.50
   Hood with a zip-out window (a fine idea, BTW) ●x175
   Distributor cap ●x6

In general, parts prices don't seem to have risen much at all for a long time: genuine competition between suppliers seems to be doing its job. One point to make is that the quality of current Triumph (and in fact many other classic) spare parts can be patchy – engine service parts are generally now made in China and are almost free, so logically they cannot also be of consistent high quality. Buy several spares of points, condensers, rotor arms, distributor caps.

Insurance
Insurance is surprisingly affordable, as classic car drivers are a very good risk and Triumphs don't attract boy racers. In the UK, get quotes from MSM, Hagerty, Adrian Flux, Footman James and others advertising in *Triumph World* and the TSSC magazine. Worldwide, consult local Triumph clubs to find a good broker. A ball park figure in the UK for an average driver might be in the ●x100-●x150 arena.

Investment potential
A good Vitesse is already a solid investment, Heralds less so. They remain usefully cheap to buy, but that has at the same time reduced their investment potential. You probably wouldn't lose money on one, but you might not gain much either. The convertibles will soon begin to appreciate quite well if they're good enough, as time ambles on and the inevitable attrition rate increases their rarity. Early Minis are substantially valuable now, which is encouraging for future early Triumph values.

The Vitesse is already doing quite well. The bigger engine and significantly better performance makes it a very attractive proposition all round. Increasing rarity is only going to help.

Vitesse production numbers are about 51,000 compared to the Herald's total of 521,000 making them rarer, and in the last year or so, around 2500 Heralds survive on the road, with 1500 Vitesses left.

The Vitesse with its small quad headlights is slightly more aggressive-looking than the Herald, the Triumph six makes the most delicious soundtrack, they're quite fast, practical, cheap to run and the dash is old-school veneer, now available in rich walnut as well as the original 1970s light teak veneers. Other than rust and dodgy early rear suspension, there's nothing not to like about them. As this sinks in with more classic car enthusiasts, the values will continue to rise.

Failings
• Single transverse rear spring suspension design on earlier cars can yield unpleasant tuck-under and a potential crash on hard cornering. Later cars (from 1967) were improved.
• Rear-end gearing without overdrive is quite low, so at motorway speeds the rpm is high: noisy and tiring, although the smaller engines in particular have no problem cruising at high revs all day. Tax cameras and congestion have reduced road speeds, so this is increasingly less of an issue. Overdrives can be found on some Vitesses.
• Rust attacks both body and chassis, although the separate chassis can make repairs easier.
• Servicing needs to be hands-on, with grease and oiling points to be attended to.
• The newest Herald/Vitesse is 48 years old.
• Over the long-term, the Vitesse gearbox and differential are not quite strong enough for the torque put out by the 2-litre six.
• Seats are 1960s: but excellent leather Miata/MX5 seats with speakers in their headrests can be substituted for the duration of your ownership.

Plus points
• Pretty.
• Fun.
• Convertible option, or useful four-seater estate or saloon bodywork.
• Pleasant to drive.
• Cheap to insure, run and repair, and an inexpensive way into the classic car world and some very entertaining events.
• Excellent exhaust chords from the six.
• Club membership will improve your social life.
• Simple enough to be fixed at home with few special tools needed.
Comprehensible wiring system and consistent Lucas wire colour code. Most Lucas problems are to do with bad earths rather than manufacturing quality.

Estate Heralds are hugely useful pieces of kit, with a very decent load space – as well as all the other benefits of an appealing classic car.

15

2 Cost considerations
– affordable, or a money pit?

Top advice is to buy the best you can afford, for a good chance of many years of trouble-free service.

Purchase
First of all, plan to buy your Triumph in the two weeks before Christmas as the discounts can be massive. This particularly applies if you want a convertible. Nobody else in the country is thinking about buying a convertible car in late December, apart from other smart people who have bought this book.

The best value to be found in the classic car world is an abandoned project. Quite a few people get to 80% of the build and either lose interest in it or are threatened with divorce, and their misfortune can be your bargain: even if the car is nearly completed, huge savings can be made.

Everybody wants to drive away in a perfect and, preferably, complete car, but you can buy an abandoned resto for maybe 20% of the money that has been avalanched into it. Downside, buying cars in boxes means some parts are inevitably missing. Upside, the missing parts for Triumphs are cheap.

Even if you don't have any experience, we recommend getting stuck in with a bargain Triumph that needs work – you'll get much more than a good car out of the process.

Having said that, for most people the best practical value for money is to buy the best example you can find. Even if you pay top dollar for what is virtually a new car, it will still only cost a fraction of what's gone into it in time and money. Many people restore cars as a hobby and sell them to fund the next rebuild – that's your top purchase option.

At the budget end of the spectrum, an entire mismatched interior can be bought and then successfully re-dyed to match. The black seat pictured here started out white.

Contact points and rotor arms cost peanuts, and work just fine if kept adjusted. They also cost 🟡x5.75 for annual replacement.

Affordable to run?

Absolutely, you're unlikely to find anything cheaper to run than a good Herald. Classic insurance, 30+mpg, hobby parts prices, skinny little cheap tyres. Engines and gearboxes are reliable, and cheap to rebuild when you wear them out. There will be welding sooner or later unless you buy a perfect resto and keep on top of paint chips, but panels are cheap and a good 130-amp MIG welder is 🟡x299.99 including VAT.

Good quality oil with enough zinc content is quite expensive in the UK, but not as expensive as an engine rebuild.

Buy the best?

Buying the best is always the smart move, as somebody else has put in much more money and time than they will get back, and you get the benefit of that.

However, if you've had the good sense to buy this book to get background information on a purchase, you're almost certainly capable of enjoying the challenge of fettling and improving a cheaper and rougher car. Go for it.

Servicing/parts costs

Not many large garages will be capable of servicing a classic car any more, and in any case it's far better and cheaper to find an individual mechanic.

Triumphs are ideal for DIY servicing, as there's nothing on the car that you can't understand. Oil change every 3000 miles with old-school oil that has enough zinc in it, check all the fluid levels, ten minutes with the grease gun, oil the trunnions, pump up the tyres and you're good to go.

Parts prices are on a par with MGs and Minis: there are enough Triumphs still on the road to generate fierce competition on parts prices – buy a copy of *Triumph World* and just enjoy running your finger down the columns of parts for peanuts. They are quite likely to cost 10% of the price of the same parts for a modern car.

Luckily for North Americans, Kendall race oil contains buckets of zinc, and is very reasonably priced.

The author's Vitesse in around 1975. Bubbling along the door bottoms isn't structural but definitely pushes down the price.

3 Living with a Herald or Vitesse

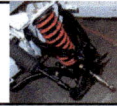

– will you get along together?

This is from the horse's mouth, as I've lived with both Heralds and Vitesses. My second ever car was a grey 1961 Herald convertible, which replaced the crashed first car, a Ford Anglia. That was back when they were just bangers rather than classics. The soft tops on Triumphs fit well enough for UK winters, and their heaters are as effective as any car heater of the period. I would happily drive my cheap-to-run convertible Triumphs through the winter, enjoying the occasional frosty sunshine country opentop run and dealing with any mechanical issues as they arose.

The author's 1965 Vitesse 6, with its silky and revvy 1600cc six, was bought in around 1975 as a daily driver because it was the nicest car available for a very reasonable price. That still applies today.

I prefer the sound and feel of the straight-six in a Vitesse, but the four-cylinder Herald is also easy, pleasant, and fun to drive. The 948cc (34.5bhp) is pretty slow by today's standards, but the 1147cc (39bhp) and 1296cc (58bhp) models are more convincing. The bigger 1596cc (70bhp) and 1998cc (95bhp and 104bhp) engines in the Vitesses have more bhp and more torque. Bhp numbers taken at max rpm are common pub chat currency, but torque is more important unless you're racing. The 948 Herald achieves a very reasonable 48lb/ft, and the MkII Vitesse gets 117lb/ft, which is definitely amusing, although harder work for its not-quite-adequate gearbox. If you like to press on a bit, the later Vitesse will do very well. Do try both engine types to experience the different flavours.

Having owned both convertible and saloon Heralds and Vitesses, I prefer the opentop option, but for city dwellers, hard tops offer much better security against thieves.

I've always been prepared to cough up a larger percentage of my income to drive cars with bigger engines and multiple cylinders, so the Triumphs I can

2-litre Vitesse is a 100mph car. Not surprising, as it's still essentially a 948cc Herald with a 2000cc engine.

remember owning have included the 1961 Herald convertible, a Herald estate, a later 1200 convertible lost to an ex (along with some lovely architectural drawings of the Alhambra), a 1600 Vitesse convertible and saloon, two 2-litre Vitesses, several Spitfires, a GT6, and a project TR6.

Having said that, I just pay more to run bigger engines, a Triumph six in good condition can return the high twenties in mpg – although not the mid-thirties that

The 1200cc engine produces 39bhp, which doesn't sound much, but with 65lb/ft of torque it can keep up with traffic.

21

Another plus point is the wooden dash on most Heralds. This one is on a Bond, but it's the same dash.

can be expected from a Herald. The soundtrack of the silky Triumph six is worth the extra.

There is plenty of room for luggage for two for weekend jaunts around the country and indeed further afield, but while you can fit four people into a Herald or Vitesse, only those in the front would enjoy a long trip. From 1961 onwards, you get a full-width wood-veneered dashboard although the seats are not leather.

Overall, any of the Herald derivatives would offer much better value and pleasure than a newer car.

Good points

It's pleasing to look at a pretty car before driving to work or anywhere else.

Home servicing and minor repairs are easy, and being hands-on with your car means you get to know it well and can head off future problems. Quietly tinkering with simple machines also reduces other life stress and makes you live longer and happier.

Vitesse gets you a much uprated dashboard, with more instruments and a nice leather-trimmed wheel.

Both the 1600cc and 2000cc Vitesse engines have a lovely silky straight-six soundtrack; there isn't much silencing.

Yet another plus point is the excellent independent front suspension design shared by all the small Triumphs.

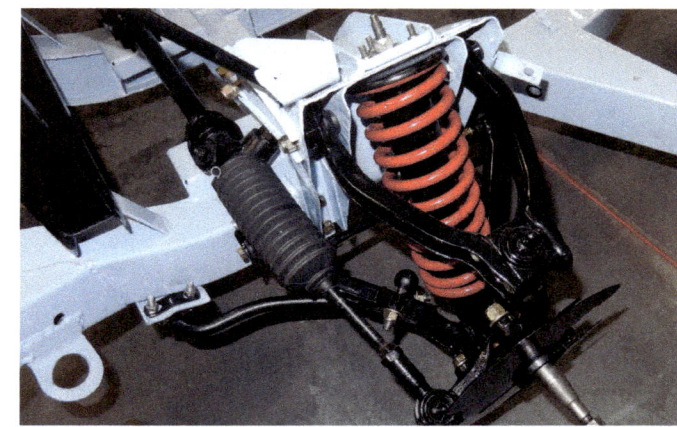

Access to the engine and front suspension via the huge flip front is the best-ever.

Access to the gearbox via the detachable gearbox cover is also very good.

The bodywork and chassis can be separated and restored at home.

MIG welding is genuinely quite easy, and the Triumphs' structure lends itself to home rust repair.

A bad point is the Herald and Vitesse 6 rear suspension. This later Rotoflex independent system is okay, but the rubbers need occasional replacement.

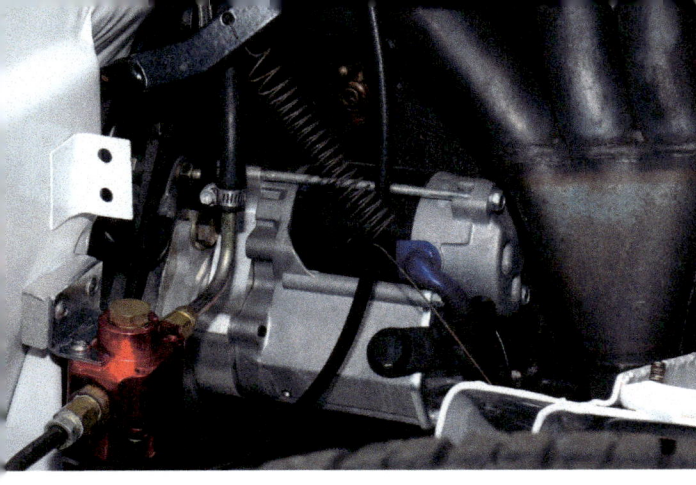

New style hi-torq starter motor is an upgrade, but the old type works well enough.

Six days, ten countries, 2319 miles: no bother for a well-sorted Herald, as *Triumph World*'s editor demonstrated.

Overdrive box on the Vitesse transforms motorway cruising with a substantial reduction in revs; cutting noise and improving fuel economy.

Spares are very cheap and readily available. Modern cars have post-warranty spares prices calculated at the max digestible stitch-up price: Triumphs do not.

The fun-per-quid ratio offered by a Herald would really be quite hard to beat. Even equally entertaining Minis and Citroën 2CVs are getting expensive now.

Bad points

The early rear suspension is a poorly conceived independent transverse-leaf-spring swing-arm design, with a fixed spring mount, which means one rear wheel can 'tuck-under' during enthusiastic cornering. If this happens, the swing axle suddenly points downwards and the back end of the car flips up on to one tyre sidewall. This is as terrifying and dangerous as it sounds, although it's only happened to me once and only because I was pushing my luck. There are cures available, though, and the later MkII (2-litre) Vitesse suspension was improved with wishbones and a flexible

Most Heralds also have appealing interior décor, but you can't really go wrong with a slab of deeply-varnished wood veneer.

drive coupling. Herald suspension was never improved by the factory, but Spitfire improvements can be retro-fitted.

Rust, more rust and yet more rust. Corrosion protection from new was poor, and rust affects both the chassis and the body structures. The rear suspension trailing arms connect to rust-prone rear outriggers, which become structurally dangerous. My Herald estate had a trailing arm break off the car due to outrigger rust, which meant three wheels attempting to steer at once: at low speed, this was just entertaining; at high speed, it would have been less so …

Here's a thought – the readily available independent diff from a Mazda MX5/Miata 1.8 is strong enough to take anything a Vitesse engine can throw at it, although creative engineering would be required to fit one.

The original gearbox cover is made of a blend of cardboard and porridge (replacements are GRP, so no worries).

Gearboxes on the Vitesse are still Herald-based rather than using the bigger and stronger gearbox that goes with the 2500cc TR6-based six. They don't last indefinitely, and gearbox parts availability, although not too bad now, will eventually evaporate. (The smaller engines in Heralds don't pose a problem for the same gearbox.) A long-term six-cylinder Triumph could usefully benefit from a Mazda/Toyota/Ford five-speed gearbox conversion.

Resting your foot on the clutch pedal wears out the thrust bearings at the back of the Triumph straight-six engines, resulting in fore and aft crank slop and an expensive repair.

Getting the big flip front and doors to fit the bodyshell well is tricky.

A rare variant that comes up occasionally is a Vitesse with an estate body: rather like the Spitfire Six, it's something special. This one is a just a Herald estate.

4 Relative values
– which model for you?

A snapshot of the Triumphs for sale in the UK in early 2019 revealed a useful picture of general values, and a few interesting related but alternative options. eBay offers some good deals, carsandclassicsforsale less so: people seem to look at the average price and think, "Let's have a go at ●x6000, that seems to be the average."

A clean Herald convertible kept in good condition is never going to lose money.

A Vitesse might cost more to buy and to fill with fuel, but other costs will be the same as a Herald. (Courtesy Paul Pannack)

Immobile projects are still available for peanuts if you join a club and keep your eyes open, but the mobile rolling resto projects start at ●x1700 for a 1970 13/60 saloon, with a claimed 75,000 miles from new with five owners. It hasn't been used

It's probably worth paying the extra for a really high quality restoration or original car, particularly with rare variants such as the coupé.

This coupé has a very nicely restored engine bay with the correct carburation and original wire air filter, which would normally have been thrown away by 1970.

for ten years but has been stored dry. The brakes are apparently not good, which makes sense – check our chapter on dealing with barn finds – but it runs and drives, and claims no rust.

Next up at ●x1890 we have a 1200 project, a drivable 1967. The passenger footwell is apparently rusty, but otherwise the seller claims it's solid. That would be worth a look: a floorpan panel from Rimmer Bros is ●x120 including VAT.

On eBay, a 1971 13/60 that "runs great but has some rust bubbles" has a starting price of ●x2150 but has attracted no bids.

●x2250 is asked for a 1967 1200 with a claimed 46,000 miles, backed up by lots of history and apparently a one-owner car, dry stored for many years and in "good condition for its age," with door rust bubbles but looking not bad.

Getting up into mainstream ready-to-drive prices we find a 1965 1200

The cardboard dash, grey steering wheel and column, white instruments, glovebox lid, and gearknob are all pedantically period-correct. Pye radio is a nice touch. This car will retain its value well.

convertible, with wire wheels, original but for a stainless exhaust and electronic ignition, claiming 93,000 miles, and it was MOT'd up to April 2018. ●x4500 is asked.

Further up the Herald status ladder at ●x8895, we're looking at a very useful 13/60 estate, with receipts for ●x10,000 in recent restoration including rust repair and fresh paint. It's a one-family car until 2016 with lots of paperwork establishing a mileage of 69,000.

Moving up to Vitesses, and they are looking like excellent value right now, with a few promising buys on offer.

●x2900 on eBay gets a red overdrive convertible MkII with MOT to April 2019. Old receipts from 2006/7 for ●x3000 suggest a credible 101,000 miles. There's a newish hood, a good interior, chromed wire wheels, but panel fit is poor which brings the price down.

Another eBay car is a 1965 Vitesse 6 at ●x3000 with the 1600 straight-six, which drives well but is unrestored and showing some 'patina.' It's been dry stored for 22 years and says 60,000 miles. There have been chassis repairs, but the sills and valances are a little frilly. That's fine, they're easy to change and the chassis is a lot more important.

A solid-looking red 1967 MkI 2-litre has been reduced to ●x5995, but there are better colours for a Vitesse.

●x4995 for a 1969 convertible MkII 2-litre with overdrive sounds reasonable. It also has a camshaft, new starter and carbs, and a pair of straight-through exhausts,

Something worth thinking about is a Bond Equipe. It's essentially a rare Herald variant with fibreglass coupé bodywork; quite expensive when new. Current values are on a par with a good Herald.

Given the design restrictions imposed by using Herald doors, the Bond is an attractive car, and yours would always be the only one at any car show.

Bond also made a later Vitesse-based car, also attractive and modern for the period with a slight wedge look to the body. Again, exterior panels are fibreglass, which doesn't prevent rust in the substructures, though certainly simplifies and cheapens repairs.

suggesting a mechanically literate owner, maybe an extra 20bhp and some future fun.

Next upwards at 🔵x6500 is a nice clean early Vitesse 6, from 1962, with a current MOT and original but for halogen headlights and a stainless exhaust, neither of which are a problem.

Top Vitesse price on this day was 🔵x10,000 from a dealer, but the car looked like nothing special.

The TSSC (Triumph Sports Car Club) is a good place for classifieds, and you should join the club anyway as there are many related benefits. The TSSC yields: a rolling resto 13/60 Herald convertible, in need of tidying but drivable and usable at 🔵x1800; a 1200 saloon with Spitfire engine and overdrive at 🔵x2500; a 1200 convertible with a new MOT and recent respray at 🔵x5950. Vitesse options are a choice of restored 1600s at 🔵x8995 and 🔵x11,000 and a good-looking solid MkII with 92,000 miles at 🔵x5250.

Going off-piste, Bonds (Heralds or Vitesses with re-styled factory GRP bodies) remain undervalued, and we find a JC Midge, a 1930-style kit car on a Spitfire base at ●x6600. These are cute, light, fast, get huge attention and are crack Triumph. I was the first to stuff a Vitesse six into a Midge and it was one of my favourite cars, retro-fitted with a Dolomite live axle to tame the wayward Triumph rear end.

On the other hand, being realistic it's much more sensible from a value point of view to avoid getting sidetracked, and to stick with the nicest Herald convertible you can afford.

www.veloce.co.uk / www.velocebooks.com
All current books • New book news • Special offers • Gift vouchers

5 Before you view
– be well informed

To avoid a wasted journey and the disappointment of finding that the car does not match your expectations, be clear about what questions you want to ask before you pick up the phone. Some of these points might appear basic, but when you're excited about the prospect of buying your new car, it's amazing how some of the most obvious things slip the mind. Also check the TSSC ads and eBay for current values.

Something else to consider, though, is that – within reason and within a reasonable range – going to inspect cars that are not as described is very useful cumulative experience. If you've seen a few rusty and worthless wrecks, you are picking up a lot of important practical knowledge about where Triumphs rust. You can also leave your phone number and an offer of fifty quid, and pick up a useful spares car in a month or two when the owner fails to sell it.

Where is the car?
You may not find a Triumph close to you, as there may only be a few for sale in a particular country or state in any one month. It's worth looking at any within reach, even if they seem unsuitable, in order to learn more.

Dealer or private sale?
Not many dealers regularly handle Triumph sports cars, although you might find something in the dealers who advertise in *Triumph World*, *Classics Monthly*, *Classic Car*, and *Classic & Sports Car*.

A private owner should have all the history, so don't be afraid to ask detailed questions. A dealer may have more limited knowledge of a car's history, but should have some documentation. A dealer may offer a warranty/guarantee (ask for a printed copy), and finance.

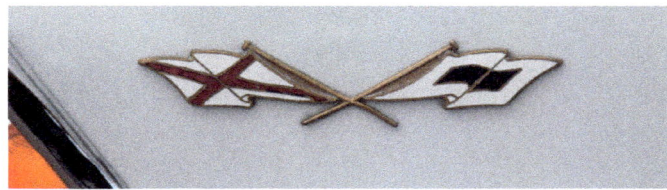

Crossed V and S flag badge is related to Vignale, and is similar to those on the Vignale-built Triumph Italia.

Cost of collection and delivery
A dealer may well be used to quoting for delivery by car transporter. A private owner may agree to meet you halfway, but only organise this after you have seen the car at the vendor's address to validate the documents.

View – when and where?
Always view at the vendor's home or business premises. In the case of a private sale, the car's documentation should tally with the vendor's name and address.

Arrange to view only in daylight and avoid a wet day. Most cars look better in poor light or when wet. Sadly, car fraud is common.

A woodrim Moto-Lita steering wheel always looks good – and looks even better if you match the wood stain colours of the rim and the dash. Mind you, Rolls didn't bother on the Corniche, and the colour mismatch looks naff.

Is late 1950s old-fashioned front styling going to rise in value faster than later updated cars? Best way to find out is to buy one.

Reason for sale

Make this one of your first questions. We don't really care why it's being sold unless the car is a dog that everybody wants rid of when its true character emerges*, but if the seller looks shifty and doesn't give a convincing answer, it's a warning flag. So why is the car being sold? How long has it been with the current owner? How many previous owners are there? If there are too many, why is that?

*You may decide to emulate Battersea Dogs' Home and rescue the dog in question, but only at the right price, and only by your own considered choice.

Condition (body/chassis/interior/mechanicals)

Ask for an honest appraisal of the car's condition over the phone, to save wasting everyone's time. Ask specifically about some of the check items that are described in Chapter 7.

Early dash and interior styling is a bit messy, and the fibreboard dash panel is nasty, frankly. However, it can be set aside and upgraded to walnut during your tenure, and sold with the car.

Matching data/legal ownership
Do VIN/chassis, engine numbers and number plate match the registration document? Is the owner's name and address recorded correctly?

For those countries that require an annual test of roadworthiness, does the car have a current document (an MOT certificate in the UK, which can be verified on 0300 123 9000 or gov.uk/check-mot-status)?

If a smog/emissions certificate is mandatory, does the car have one? If required, does the car carry a current road fund licence or licence plate tag? Does the vendor own the car outright? Money might be owed to a finance company or bank: the car (or its engine) could even be stolen! Several organisations will supply information, based on the car's licence plate number or VIN number, for a fee. Such companies can often also tell you whether the car has been written-off by an insurance company.

In the UK these organisations can supply vehicle data:
DVSA 0300 123 9000
HPI 0845 300 8905
AA 0344 209 0754
DVLA 0844 306 9203
RAC 0800 015 6000
Other countries will have similar organisations.

Unleaded fuel
Has the cylinder head been modified to run on unleaded fuel? Triumph engines will eventually all need hardened valve seats fitted, unless they are used very lightly.

Insurance
Check with your existing insurer before setting out to buy a Triumph, as your current policy might not cover you to drive the car if you do buy it.

How you can pay
A cheque/check will take several days to clear and the seller may prefer to sell to a cash buyer. A wad of waved fifties is very tempting to a seller. A banker's draft (a cheque issued by a bank) is theoretically as good as cash: invite the seller to accompany you to your bank when collecting it, to reassure them it's a real one. There are fake banker's drafts about, so while it's safer to pay with one than to carry cash, it's less safe to accept one as payment.

Buying at auction?
If the intention is to buy at auction, see Chapter 10 for further advice. Triumphs tend not to come up at mainstream car auctions very often.

Professional vehicle check (mechanical examination)
For production cars, there are often marque/model specialists who will undertake professional examination of a vehicle on your behalf. The owners' clubs are key – the owners know the cars inside out and are happy to help out prospective new club members, usually for free or for beer. Taking a car for an MOT as part of your test drive is also well worthwhile. If the owner refuses to let the car go for an MOT, maybe don't buy it.

Period radios look very cool, and can now be secretly upgraded to Bluetooth and MP3, with good speakers mounted in boxes under the dash – there's plenty of room.

www.veloce.co.uk / www.velocebooks.com
All current books • New book news • Special offers • Gift vouchers

6 Inspection equipment
– these items will really help

This book
Reading glasses (if you need them for close work)
Torch or flashlight
Probe (a small screwdriver works very well)
Overalls
Digital camera or phone/selfie stick
Cloth-wrapped magnet for finding body filler
A sensible friend, ideally from the local Triumph club
A disappointed expression

Before you rush out of the door, gather together a few items that will help as you work your way around the car. This book is designed to be your guide at every step, so take it along and use the check boxes to help you assess each area of the car you're interested in. Let the seller see you using it.

Take reading glasses if you need them to read documents and make close-up inspections. A torch or flashlight with fresh batteries will be useful for peering into the wheel-arches and under the car.

A small screwdriver can be used – with care – as a probe, to check for body and chassis rust.

Be prepared to get dirty. Take along a pair of overalls, if you have them. Fixing a mirror or phone/camera at an angle on the end of a

Reading specs not only allow you to focus, they can help prevent rust getting in your eyes when you're poking about under a potential purchase.

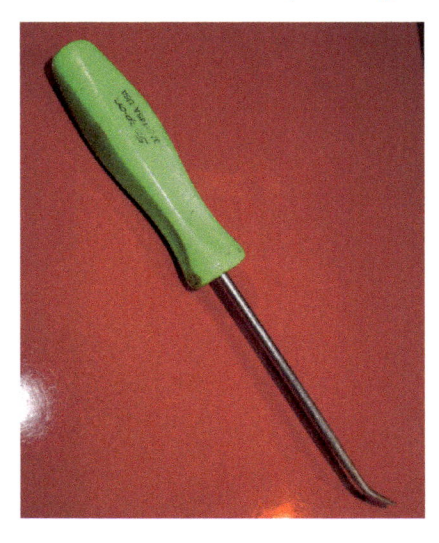

A probe is useful for poking at rust bubbles. Take care, though – the seller won't be impressed if you turn small bubbles into gaping holes.

38

stick may seem odd, but it's very useful for checking the condition of the underside, pipework, etc. It will also help you to peer into some of the important crevices.

Take overalls because you will be under the car. They don't need to be branded: these good-quality overalls were flogged off cheap by the Bentley club because Bentley owners are generally no longer hands-on.

If you have the use of a digital camera, take it along so that you can study some areas of the car more closely later. A current smartphone camera will do almost as well. Take a picture of any part of the car that raises concerns, and seek knowledgeable opinions.Ideally, have an experienced friend or enthusiast accompany you. Joining a Triumph club will yield many such friends.

The disappointed facial expression is a useful buying tool: even if you're gagging to buy the car, express continuous visible and audible doubts about its value and desirability when beating down the price.

The smartphone now optionally replaces the torch, the mirror and the camera – just light up and shoot away wherever you can reach. Duct-taping it to a ruler is better than buying a selfie stick, which would just be embarrassing if you're older than 13.

Serious light underneath a car you're inspecting is still well worthwhile. Rechargeable LED trouble lights are remarkably powerful.

7 Fifteen minute evaluation
– walk away or stay?

Paperwork
Correct paperwork is critically important in the UK: if the car is not registered absolutely correctly, it could finish up as an undrivable ornament next time you take it for an MOT test. The VIN and engine numbers should tally with the registration book. If it has a 'Q' plate it's already registered as a collection of assorted parts so it should be okay. Note that many people don't like the non-changeable Q plates, affecting values.

Doors get rusty along the bottoms. ●x150 gets you a new door skin, while ●x35 buys a door bottom repair panel, leaving the other ●x115 for a secondhand MIG welder. (Courtesy Keith Evans)

The front bumper irons are also the hinges for the flip front, and are rather vulnerable. Check that they're not bent. (Courtesy Keith Evans)

A check to see if the car is stolen is also wise.

In most of the USA, the registration and testing regime is simple, but emissions can be an issue in some states.

Exterior, bodywork

Check for body panel fit. Back off a few paces and just look at the fit of bonnet, boot, and doors. The big flip front and the doors are quite tricky to align with each other and with the body tub, so study the panel gaps. Don't expect too much precision: 1960s Triumphs rarely fit together very precisely.

Check the paint for micro-blisters, fisheyes, bubbles, chips, and a smoothness of line along the main body panels. Look inside panels for filler and overspray. The next buyer will knock money off, so you should as well.

Wrap a magnet in a clean soft cloth and run it over the rust-prone areas of the car, particularly the lower half. If it's made of rolled up *Daily Mirrors*, chicken wire and porridge, the magnet won't stick to it.

Look for evidence of repaired damage. On a chassis-based car it's less of a worry than on a monocoque, but it still lowers the car's value.

Check underneath for visible chassis damage and rust, and if anything worries you, measure diagonally across the frame to check straightness. Bear in mind that it may not have been quite straight when new, and that it may not matter much if the suspension has been aligned to suit: these are old cars. If anything worries you, walk away, or deduct the cost of replacement chassis parts and welding.

The big bonnet panel rusts in the corners, and it's quite difficult to adjust to make it fit well. This one has a lock; a useful mod. Obscure fact: the M stands for Michelotti.

42

Build quality
If you're considering an expensive restored car, look at the brake and fuel lines and their securing clips in the engine bay and under the car. This section of a restoration is a boring and time-consuming task, and it can be carried out in two ways: impatiently, by someone who's rushing to finish the car; or detailed and perfect, with smooth piping bends and equidistant spaced clips, fitted by an anal-retentive, picky engineer type. Do the pipes and clips say the build is sloppy and careless? If you're not prepared to rebuild such a car again to get it done properly, walk away. If you do want to rebuild it, make an insultingly low offer that reflects the 300 hours of work you'll have to do.

Interior
There isn't really much interior involved in a Triumph, and it's all easy to fit, apart from seat skins which require patience (and will involve bleeding and bandages). You can buy budget interior kits, or really good, but more expensive, items from Newton Commercial. For the purposes of knocking down a buying price, ●x1500 would be the ballpark cost of a nice new interior.

Interior condition is straightforward to check, but sit in the seats to check the firmness of the seat foams, and check all the instruments. Nothing wrong here at all. (Courtesy Keith Evans)

Gearbox
The gear change movement should be crisp and in the shape of an H rather than a sloppy V. There should be no unusual amount of noise in any gear, and the car should not jump out of gear.

Engine

Look for the correct amount of engine oil that's not thin and black. Listen for rattles when the engine is started cold, look for any smoke from the exhaust, and in the six-cylinder engine in particular, look at the crankshaft by the pulley while somebody pushes down the clutch pedal to see if there is any fore and aft crank movement, indicating possibly terminal engine block wear.

Check the oil and coolant for head gasket emulsion mayonnaise. Thin, black engine oil indicates neglect, and is a warning sign.

8 Key points
– where to look for problems

- Body and paintwork – you can usually find a few faults
- Wipers – check action and condition, as geometry and rack lubrication can be dodgy
- Glass, lights – quite cheap to replace, but worth complaining about faults
- Wheels – check wheels and tyres inside and outside for kerbing damage, cuts, defects and the age of the tyres. They should be scrapped at seven years old, even if they have plenty of tread, because the rubber goes hard and grip decreases
- Rolling gear – check wheel bearings, steering and suspension joints for play

Even if they have good tread, tyres last a maximum seven years. Visible cracking means you don't even risk driving home on them.

- Interior condition – visual inspection, check seat runner function
- Electrical functions – check that everything works. Triumph wiring is simple to fix but faults reduce value
- Instrumentation – check for function and accuracy
- Engine – listen for rattles from cold, check for whitish emulsion in oil and water, check cooling system, check for reasonably fresh oil, check the cylinder compressions (a tester costs about ●x20)
- Transmission – Check for gearbox noise, sloppy gearlever bushes, jumping out of gear
- Rear axle/diff – Leaks or noises?
- Cooling system/radiator condition? Electric fan fitted? Shrouding condition? Quality?
- Exhaust Any rust or leaks? Condition of mountings?
- Brakes – pulling evenly? Does the front lock up first as it should? Handbrake function ok?

Extra instrumentation is the sign of a very enthusiastic owner, which is a good thing. RPM, air temp, clock, hygrometer, voltmeter: all occasionally useful.

Mileage? Who knows. It's easy to fake unless you have a documented history from day one. Check the function of all the instruments.

Rock the wheel to check wheel bearings; look at the suspension bushes and brake callipers and pads. The kingpins need oil, not grease. Does the owner know that?

- Steering rack and joints – any slop? Are the front tyres unevenly worn, suggesting tracking/geometry problems? Does the steering self-centre? If not, castor is wrong (usually adjustable unless chassis is bent)
- Suspension – shocks ok? Does the car sit evenly on its springs? Is the back sagging?

9 Serious evaluation
– 60 minutes for years of enjoyment

Viewing and inspecting a classic Triumph involves peeking into nooks and crannies looking for corrosion, wear, and bodges that have occurred over decades and maybe a hundred thousand miles. You might end up keeping the car for many years, so a few hours spent on a really careful examination will pay off.

Use this chapter to calculate a score for each car you examine.

Score each section using the boxes as follows: 4 = Excellent; 3 = Good; 2 = Average; 1 = Poor. The totting-up procedure is explained at the end of the chapter. Be realistic in your marking!

Avoid DIY amputations
Don't take any risks when examining a car. In particular, don't rely on a jack to hold it up. Get the car up on a pair of ramps, wheels chocked and in gear, or supported on axle stands, before getting under it.

Exterior [4] [3] [2] [1]
Any baggy old disaster of a car looks great at night and in the rain, so that's when you don't buy one. Always look at a car in daylight, and, if possible, back it halfway into a garage, crouch down and look along the body sides towards the light – any peculiarities will show up. A weird but effective way of examining a car is to hand-wash it: the seller will be puzzled but is unlikely to turn down the offer. Your hands quite often pick up anomalies, and during the process you will naturally examine every inch of the bodywork with your eyes as well as your fingers.

Don't ever put anything you want to use again, such as your arm or your head, under a car unless it is supported on axle stands. Hydraulic jacks can leak, fail, and fall over.

Bodywork symmetry and fit is variable in old Triumphs. If there are ripples and bumps and the panels don't fit very well, knock down the price, or move on and find a better car if the visual details really bother you. The feel and character of the whole car is probably more important than the precision of the panel gaps; once you've looked at a few Triumphs you'll know what your priorities are.

Old steel production cars can be piles of dangerously corroded scrap, beautifully and expertly reconstructed with newspaper and body filler. This applies less to cars with a proper chassis, but it still applies. Magnets stick to metal but not to filler. Filler over a visibly solid steel repair is variably acceptable depending on the asking price.

Reason for sale
The condition and specifications of the car are much more important than what somebody tells you about why they're selling it, but if the car is dodgy and being moved on for bad reasons, you might smell a rat by probing the owner a little. If you gaze thoughtfully at people and keep quiet, they will quite often start babbling and will tell you much more than they wanted to.

One aspect of classic car life is that a surprisingly large number of people simply love restoring cars, but can't be bothered with driving them: they regard the whole thing as a jigsaw puzzle, and lose interest as soon as it's finished.

Some people just go sour on the whole long and expensive rebuilding process and find that the fun has gone out of it, leaving a bargain for the next owner.

Yet more find that there is a price to pay when you abandon non-petrolhead partners to watch *Coronation Street* on their own, while spending a year of evenings and weekends in the garage, without keeping domestic bliss supported with new sofas, kitchens and some quality attention. The choice can then be between divorce or getting rid of the xxxxxx project. As a buyer, you might feel guilty about snatching the resulting divorce-sourced bargain … but the guilt will soon pass.

Legalities
Any problem that arises with paperwork not being entirely kosher can be a big issue. If it's a project banger, you might be tempted not to bother. However, after you've put five grand and two years into it, the car is no longer a banger, but dodgy paperwork can still arise and bite you. Stolen or part-stolen cars can be impounded and crushed, or returned to a previous owner.

The address where you buy the car should be the one in the registration documents, the VIN number or chassis number should tally with the car, the engine number should be correct, and ideally you would get receipts and paperwork going way back, supporting the mileage claimed on the speedo.

Cars rebuilt with period registrations and a new chassis number are fine: of my own Triumphs, one was a kit car based on a J-registered tax-free 1971 Triumph Vitesse which is now a Triumph Midge, re-registered with a new SAB TVRO chassis number. All of my cars have been correctly registered according to contemporary rules, so I've never had a problem.

A Q registration number prefix means a car has been assembled from assorted bits and pieces, and apart from being rare and rather interesting, is no problem at all provided all the numbers still tally. It drops the car's price, as many people don't like it and it can't be changed once issued.

There are many thieves and conmen operating in the secondhand car market, and buying a dodgy Triumph would be an expensive mistake.

An HPI check is wise, as a significant and disappointing percentage of secondhand British cars have something dodgy in their pasts: it would be upsetting to buy a nice car and then find out that it still belongs to somebody else.

Different rules apply worldwide and in different states and provinces. Emissions can be a problem in some provinces and states in North America, but generally anything that is registered and street-legal will remain registered and street-legal.

Engine and chassis numbers
The chassis number should match the registration document, and the engine number should also tally with it. We don't care much if it's the 'correct' engine

49

number, although in the USA there is something of a fetish for matching engine numbers – but we do care if the engine turns out to have been stolen.

In the UK, old engines (pre-1972) have no emission rules other than not emitting visible smoke, so you can run all Heralds and Vitesses with open pipes, evil camshaft profiles and a forest of Webers for decidedly nippy performance at the expense of dreadful emissions and upsetting the polar bears.

Unleaded fuel

Many engines built before about 1976 don't have hardened exhaust valve seats. That includes Herald and Vitesse engines. The seats are cut directly into the cast iron of the heads, which was previously the usual practice for ordinary cars using leaded petrol, and the valve seats will slowly erode. Other BMC – Austin, Morris, MG, etc – engines are probably worse: Triumph engines can sometimes last for a lot longer. Rumour says that Triumph management was better at internal BMC company politics, so they got higher quality cast iron for their engines and cylinder heads.

Before about 1976, exhaust ports were cut directly into the metal of the head, and unleaded fuel will erode them. This is the new replacement valve seat, hardened to suit modern fuel. Has this job been done on the car you're thinking of buying?

The author took the opportunity to smooth the ports in his Vitesse head for more power while the new unleaded valve seats went in, as the cylinder head was off anyway.

The area of the head that suffers from erosion ends up being cut out anyway when hard seats are eventually fitted, so there's no need to worry about it until you lose power, which happens when you finally run out of compression. It's more money off your offer price, though, unless there's proof that the valve seats have been upgraded.

Insurance
Before road-testing a car, make very sure that either your own insurance covers you for driving other cars, or that the seller's insurance covers "any driver" and is current.

Oil and coolant
The dipstick tells a whole story. If the oil is low, thin, runny and black, the car has been neglected. You need to see the correct level of fairly clean oil on the dipstick.

Take the oil filler cap off: if there's a lot of whitish emulsion inside it, there's water in the oil, which suggests that a head-gasket is gone or the block or cylinder head is warped. A little emulsion is okay, as it tends to suggest internal condensation and a rarely-used engine. The coolant cap tells the same story – if there's a lot of white kak in the cap and the radiator, there's water in the oil. At best it's a head-off job to replace a failed gasket, at worst it's an engine rebuild.

(**Caution!** Remember to check the radiator cap while the engine is cold. If you take it off while the engine's hot, the steam will instantly boil your head.)

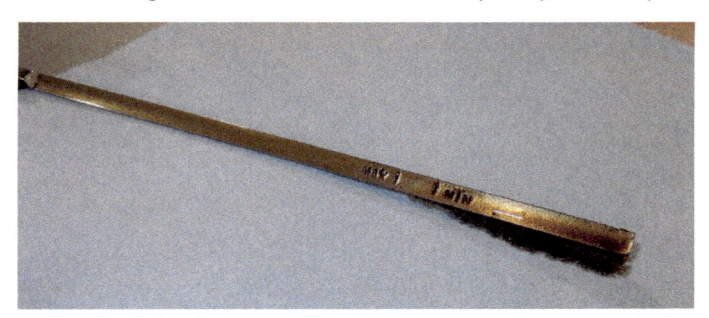

The dipstick tells a story. You want to see the right amount of oil, and of about this colour. If it's black and runny it hasn't been changed, which means the car has been neglected.

Compression test
Even cylinder compression numbers are a good guide to a sound engine. A compression tester costs about ●x20 and is screwed into each sparkplug hole in turn, with the ignition disconnected and the throttle pedal floored while spinning the engine. The numbers should be within 10% of each other, and that is more important than the actual numbers. Low compression on one cylinder could be a serious piston problem, or a less serious valve, head gasket, or cylinder head problem. In which case, budget for some engine work, or walk away.

Cold start and hot idle
If the engine is worn, starting it from stone cold is a good way to hear any clattering or tapping from excessive bearing clearances or other wear. Having said that, in

the Triumph 6, the oil tends to drain right back down into the sump after a period of disuse, leaving the bearings dry, which results in an appalling 'death rattle' when the engine starts. Astonishingly, these engines can do this for years, and somehow they stay in one piece. I know of one engine that achieved 400,000 miles after it started rattling at 50,000 miles.

Usefully, the fuel also drains back to the fuel tank over time, and if you stick to a mechanical fuel pump, there is usually oil pressure in the engine by the time fuel reaches the carbs and the engine fires. For cars with electric fuel pumps, a secret pump switch left turned off until the oil has circulated is a good idea, and is also good thief protection.

You need to leave the car idling until it reaches normal operating temperature and more if it's going to overheat, and then you want to hear the electric fan coming in (if the car has one fitted) and to watch the temperature stabilizing. Keep the bonnet closed during this test, as an open bonnet is a good aid to cooling.

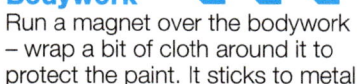

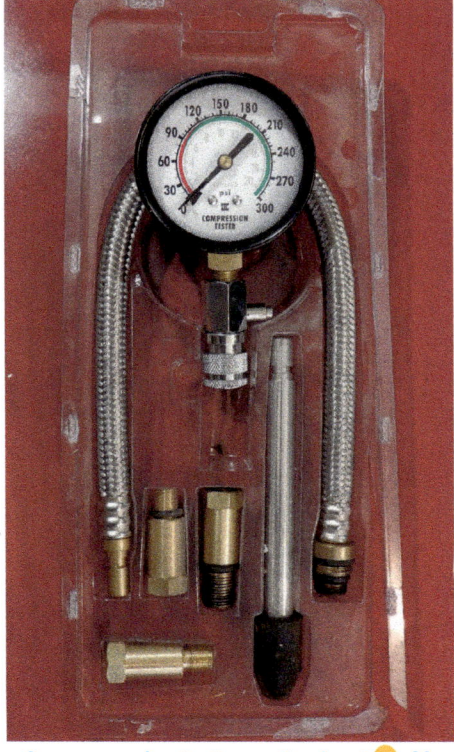

A compression tester costs about ●x20: good and even compressions (within about 10%) tell you the engine is healthy. One low cylinder could mean a rebuild. A very big discount, or walk away.

Bodywork ④ ③ ② ①

Run a magnet over the bodywork – wrap a bit of cloth around it to protect the paint. It sticks to metal and falls off if there's deep filler. The sills and valances on the Herald and Vitesse are not structurally critical and don't need to be solid. They're also cheap, and new ones just bolt on. Filler in the rear bodywork and on the chassis (yes, I've seen that) is more of an issue.

Floors, the boot floor, and the chassis outriggers are tricky and expensive repairs, and just a few paint bubbles means nastiness beneath. If you see a bubble, that usually means secret rust for six inches around the bubble. My last Mini (RIP) had a shiny paint job over a lot of filler, and was actually named Bubble as the rust erupted.

Superficially, look for rust at the bottom back edges of the bonnet, and at the bottom of the door skins and the door frames. The battery box suffers from acid attack, and the area around the base of the brake and clutch master cylinders rusts after brake fluid spills remove the paint. The screen pillars on open cars rot under the rubbers: a tricky repair. The rear wheel arches are vulnerable to extensive post-paint-chip rust.

Chassis   [4] [3] [2] [1]
Damage is actually more likely to be found than serious rust on a chassis, if the body of the inspected Triumph is good. The back of the chassis is less well protected by historically leaked oil from the engine and gearbox. Outriggers crumble and the front beam by the bonnet hinges tends to get bent. The chassis lasts quite well as far as rusting goes, and luckily there are still plenty of spares around with club members. A new chassis is not available but another good secondhand one generally is, and many chassis sections are still available.

Wheels and tyres   [4] [3] [2] [1]
The condition of wheels and tyres can tell you a lot. First, check the insides as well as the outsides of both rims and tyres for damage or bulges. Check the age of the tyres: there's a code number on the sidewalls. Google "tyre age code" to find the info for your country. Tyres should not be used for more than six or seven years, particularly in higher-performance cars, although if they're kept on a lightweight car in a dark garage and used regularly enough to avoid flat-spotting damage they can last longer. (The actual problem is that they eventually go hard and lose grip.)

Fortunately, replacing old tyres for our Triumphs is quite cheap, as they're small. Crossplies or bias belted tyres are correct up to about 1970. If you prefer radial tyres, I've seen a set of five newly-manufactured old-school 145 x 13 Pirelli Cinturatos for ●x400, which means ●x80 each. Not bad for specialized replica tyres. Crossplies are similarly priced. Don't go much bigger than the standard 520 x 13 for Heralds and 560 x 13 for the Vitesse, or 145 x 13 and 155 x 13 for radial tyres. That gets the right weight on the tyre's road contact patch. If you're changing tyre type from radials to crossply or vice versa, front wheel tracking should be 1/8th to 1/16th toe-in for crossply/bias ply tyres, zero toe-in for radials. Essentially, old-school crossply tyres lose grip quite quickly in a corner but do so more controllably, whereas radials grip better but then lose grip more violently. The Herald family was originally designed for lower-grip crossply tyres, and paradoxically it may be the increased grip of better tyres that causes the rear axle to jack up.

Wear patterns on tyres can tell you quite a lot. If tyres are worn in the middle or on both outside edges, that means poor maintenance, incorrect tyre air pressures and a careless or ill-informed owner. Over-inflation makes the tyre bulge into a bagel shape so it only runs on the balding middle area of the tread, and under-inflation means it's squashy and flat so the outer edges wear more quickly.

If one inside or outside edge of the front tyre tread is worn much more than the middle and the other side, the wheels are not running parallel and are probably either pointing too far inwards or outwards. This is usually a simple adjustment of the front tracking, and not a worry if a tracking check confirms that they were out of adjustment. If the tyres are worn on one side and the tracking checks out to be correct, there could be a camber issue.

Camber is how far out the bottom of the wheel is from the car, compared to the top of the wheel: a little negative camber (wheels sloping inwards at the top) is good, because the tyre deforms slightly into a more desirable shape on cornering. When the car is stuffed into a left-hand corner with enthusiasm and a little negative camber, centrifugal forces compete with grip to make the right front tyre tread sit flat on the road. Lots of negative camber gets you better cornering, but the downside is that on the straight, the tyres are not running vertically so the inside edge wears faster than the outside edge. On Minis, one degree of negative camber is a good compromise between tyre wear and grip, so that may help as a guide.

If just one tyre (of a matched pair on either axle) is worn on the outside or inside, that suggests the suspension on that corner is bent or otherwise out of true. That wheel is at the wrong angle compared to the rest. If the rear tyres are worn unevenly, the suspension is either tired, damaged, or out of true.

These problems can simply be maladjustment, but a full alignment check would be very useful before buying the car. If you're serious about buying a car and you suspect it has suspension alignment issues, a full check is definitely worth doing. Usually there will be enough adjustment in the suspension to get both ends straightened out, but if not, you're looking at some relatively major work. It can be done, but check the potential cost before making your offer.

Brakes [4] [3] [2] [1]

Check the brake discs for wear and condition, where fitted. You can't check for warped discs by looking, but pulsing at the pedal in time with wheel rotation can mean warped discs. Not a big deal, but more money off the price, please. Ask the owner to demonstrate the brakes somewhere safe, and see if you're happy with the stopping power, and that the car stops in a straight line.

You may not want to keep the standard servo, if there is one fitted: I once had to remove a Vitesse brake servo because the front wheels seemed to lock as soon as the pedal was touched.

Check for brake fluid leaks: this one is seeping and oil should be visible on the brake backplates. Some Triumphs have only a single brake circuit and no low fluid level warning ...

Suspension [4] [3] [2] [1]

You're looking for saggy coil springs, broken leaves on the rear leaf springs, and leaks from the shock absorbers. Bouncing each corner of the car will tell you whether the shocks are working. Check that old rubber bushes haven't turned to carbon kak. Nylon suspension bushes are harder and make the suspension sharper, but can give a harsher ride.

Drivability [4] [3] [2] [1]

When evaluating the performance and handling of the car, go for a ride first as a passenger – the owner will normally be happy to show you how well the car goes. When you drive the car yourself, you're not looking for its limits, you're judging whether you will still enjoy it when the novelty has worn off.

Electrics
This is nice and simple. Either things work or they don't. However, if you see Scotchloks in the wiring, that's a sign of amateur butchery and future serious problems: a mechanic friend of mine is happy to repair corroded or broken wiring, but if he sees a Scotchlok, he says either this car gets a complete rewire or just take it away. Also, look for tidiness and a neatly wrapped wiring loom in restored cars, and check behind the dashboard for either clipped neatness or a mass of multi-coloured spaghetti. (The original and correct Triumph behind-dash tagliatelle is a bit of a mess, to be fair.)

Take a tape or CD to check out the sound system. You won't be able to hear it much over the slipstream in a convertible, but it's another thing over which to chew your lip and look doubtful.

Restoration quality
Restorers can be amateurish or just amateur, and you're going to get the same variability of workmanship as with any DIY work: if you look at how the car is assembled and can see the equivalent of a shelf duct-taped to a wall, you can either walk away or regard the car in front of you as a temporarily assembled collection of pieces that will need to be taken apart and then put together properly. Make an offer based on that judgement, or stroll away.

The restorer may have done things like re-using Nylocks: if you don't know what that means, educate yourself about single-use fasteners before you consider buying or rebuilding an old car.

Look under the car at the piping, which is a good clue as to general build quality. The fuel and brake lines are secured by clips. Are they equally spaced? Are there plenty of them, and are they the right size? Has the piping itself been carefully bent around jam-pots, jack-handles, and so on in a pleasing set of neat bends, or is it all a bit haphazard where it's not on public view?

Fuel system
Check for leaks, for neat and well-made fuel piping, and for silicone sealer used anywhere near the fuel system. (This dissolves in the fuel and then reappears later as gorilla snot in the carbs.)

SUs and the Stromberg carbs usually used on Triumphs are cheap, simple and effective, while Italian twin-chokes with polished trumpets are much more glamorous: but if they don't already run well, tuning them is like herding cats. Overfuelling from Webers can ruin a smaller engine.

Many Triumph enthusiasts have traditionally 'upgraded' from Stromberg to SU carbs, but it was intriguing and surprising to find that career Triumph restorer Randy Zoller of British Heritage in San Diego would ideally use three Strombergs (with fresh diaphragms) on his theoretical ultimate 2-litre Triumph six. Perfect fuel delivery, apparently. I've always thought Strombergs were just fine, and never felt the need to change them on any of my Triumphs: looks like I was right.

Methods of payment
It's risky wandering around with a big wad of cash these days, but flourishing a lot of banknotes is a powerful buying tool. Visible cash is very tempting, in small denominations to create a fat and satisfying wad, and the price is still flexible up to the moment when you hand it over. Just be aware of your location.

Bank drafts are a safe way to pay, but there are fakes around so I would no longer let a car be driven away unless I had seen a draft being issued at a bank. Other people may begin to think this way. If you buy from a dealer, using a credit card is wise as it offers some useful protection.

Offering to pay for the fuel used in a long test run is a good idea: it says you're serious about buying the car, and it makes a long test run a reasonable request.

Take it for an inspection

Most countries have some sort of a tech inspection system, and it's mostly state-run and good value compared to a private inspection. For Brits, the MOT test is excellent value for anybody buying any car. ●x55 gets you a good mechanical going-over, up on a ramp where you can usually, unofficially, join the examiner under the car and get a good look at everything. It's a rare treat for an MOT tester to get to look at something interesting rather than his daily diet of baggy BMWs, and for his expertise to be valued and respected, so a classic Triumph will get his full attention.

The UK's MOT test covers the body and vehicle structure, steering, suspension, brakes, emissions, windscreen, wipers/washers, lighting, door/bonnet/boot operation, seatbelts, seat mountings, mirrors, horn, exhaust system condition and noise level, fuel system, tyres, wheels, and registration plates.

While MOT testers' expertise is pretty variable, any serious problems are likely to be spotted, together with worn or damaged suspension components, uneven brakes, fluid leaks, damage to tyres and wheels on the insides, insecure brake or fuel lines and many other things that you might have missed during your own inspection.

If the car passes the test, that's good news, and the price should be unaffected – surely the seller expected it to be roadworthy in the first place?

If it fails, the seller is at a psychological disadvantage and has no good reason for not adjusting the price downwards to reflect the cost of the repairs. An extra bonus of going through a government test as part of examining a car is that the garage's computer may well flag up anything dodgy in the car's registration if the paper bumf is not kosher, which ideally you need to know before, rather than after, you've bought the car.

Carpets and trim [4] [3] [2] [1]

This is either in good condition or not. A basic home retrim will run between ●x1000 and ●x1500 in vinyl, although an excellent wheeze is to collect a complete and very cheap secondhand replacement interior in random colours, and then re-dye it all in a new colour of your choice. This is surprisingly easy and looks much better than you would expect. The vinyl was dyed in the first place, so re-dyeing it works just fine.

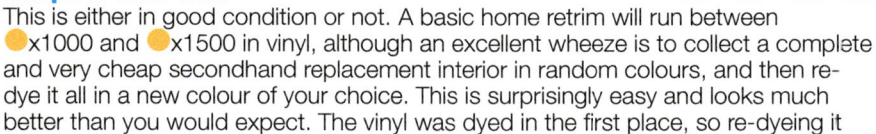

For a Herald or a Vitesse, an upgrade to leather trim, or at least leather seat facings, would be a good match for the upscale veneered interior woodwork of the cars, but something to consider for the longer term is that black and dark-coloured leather looks more inviting with age and patina, whereas magnolia leather doesn't.

Here's where the Herald family rusts. With the painted parts, you're looking for bubbles, and looking and feeling behind the panels for filler and rust. With the chassis members, you're entitled to give them a good poke with a screwdriver to see if they're solid.

The sills were not rust-protected at the factory, but they are cheap and available, and just bolt in place. No worries at all, unless there's nothing left to bolt them to.

The door bottoms rust out, beginning at the back. This one is just starting to bubble. A relatively easy repair with MIG welder and sheet steel.

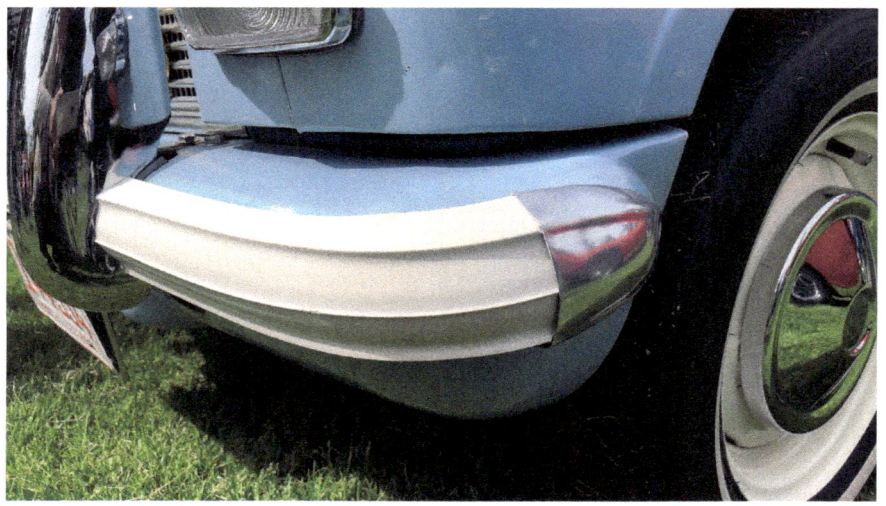

The bottom corners of the flip-up bonnet are vulnerable to rust and also to damage: it's rare for a Herald or Vitesse to retain a good fit between bonnet and bumpers.

The bootlid rusts along the bottom. Either find a better secondhand panel, or again it's quite an easy repair in flat sheet steel.

The chrome parts of the rear bumpers rust from the inside. The main bumper panels under the trim valances are also vulnerable, though easy to replace.

Empty the boot, take out the carpet and check the floor of the spare wheel well.

Battery acid leaking over 50 years or so can corrode the bulkhead beneath the battery. It's worth a look underneath.

The clutch and brake fluid is corrosive, and there is often body rust around the cylinders from spillage over the years.

Under the bonnet: the front chassis beam can become bent from minor parking impacts, and the body support outriggers rust where flying stones chip the paint.

The front outriggers can rust from the inside out as well as from old stone damage chipping the paint.

On British cars, the outriggers are likely to be worse on the gutter side of the car.

The floor panels crumble under damp carpet, particularly on the less water-repellent convertible cars. New floor panels are cheap, and it's a relatively easy repair.

The rear outriggers also rust, and they carry the suspension trailing arms, so a failure sets one of the rear wheels free to steer the car where it wants. These outriggers need to be solid.

Boot floor, spare wheel well, and bumper outriggers also frequently require repair, but it's usually possible without much dismantling.

Evaluation procedure
Add up the total points.
Score: 60 = excellent; 45 = good; 30 = average; 15 = poor.
Cars scoring over 42 will be completely usable and will require only maintenance and care to preserve condition. Cars scoring between 15 and 31 will require some serious work (at much the same cost regardless of score). Cars scoring between 32 and 41 will require very careful assessment of the necessary repair/restoration costs in order to arrive at a realistic value.

10 Auctions
– sold! Another way to buy your dream

It's quite rare for a Triumph to come up at a general car auction, but they come up regularly at classic car auctions. You could save thousands so it's worth keeping your eyes on the auction listings via the internet.

A later Herald fitted with the estate body has to be an excellent choice for a classic weekend fun car that's also very useful. With no airbags or intrusive crash structures, it offers as much load space as many current obese SUV designs.
(Courtesy Keith Evans)

Auctions – pros & cons
Pros: Prices will usually be lower than those of dealers and sometimes private sellers, and you might grab a real bargain on the day. Auctioneers have usually established clear title with the seller. At the venue you can usually examine documentation relating to the vehicle.
Cons: You have to rely on a sketchy catalogue description of condition & history. The opportunity to inspect is limited and you cannot drive the car. Auction cars are often a little below par and may require some work. It's easy to get carried away and overbid. There will usually be a buyer's premium to pay in addition to the auction hammer price.

You can't drive a car at an auction, although if there is a serious defect that becomes immediately apparent the auctioneers may have to become involved in resolving the issue.

Which auction?
Established auctioneers advertise in car magazines and on the auction houses' websites. A catalogue, or a simple printed list of the lots for auctions, might only be available a day or two ahead, though often lots are listed and pictured on auctioneers' websites much earlier. Contact the auction company to ask if previous auction selling prices are available, as this is useful information (details of past sales are often available on websites).

Catalogue, entry fee and payment details
When you buy the catalogue of the vehicles in the auction, it often acts as a ticket allowing two people to attend the viewing days and the auction. Catalogue details tend to be comparatively brief, but will include information such as "one owner from new, low mileage, full service history," etc. It will also usually show a guide price to give you some idea of what to expect to pay, and will tell you what is charged as a 'buyer's premium.' The catalogue will also contain details of acceptable forms of payment. At the fall of the hammer an immediate deposit is usually required, the balance payable within 24 hours. If the plan is to pay by cash there may be a cash limit. Some auctions will accept payment by debit card. Sometimes credit or charge cards are acceptable, but they will often incur an extra charge. A bank draft or bank transfer will have to be arranged in advance with your own bank as well as with the auction house. No car will be released before all payments are cleared. If delays occur in payment transfers, storage costs can accrue.

Buyer's premium
A buyer's premium will be added to the hammer price: don't forget this in your calculations. It is not usual for there to be further tax on the purchase price and/or on the buyer's premium in the UK.

Viewing
In some instances it's possible to view on the day, or days before, as well as in the hours prior to, the auction. There are auction officials available who will help out by opening engine and luggage compartments and to allow you to inspect the interior. While the officials may start the engine for you, a test drive is out of the question. Crawling under and around the car as much as you want is permitted, but you can't suggest that the car you are interested in be jacked up, or attempt to do that yourself. Use smartphone cameras to look underneath and in crevices. You can also ask to see any documentation available.

You can listen to the engine at an auction, and have a look at the colour and amount of oil in it, both of which yield very useful information about previous maintenance standards.

Bidding
Before you take part in the auction, decide your maximum bid – and stick to it!
 Take a friend equipped with a sharp object and orders to stab you if you get carried away. It may take a while for the auctioneer to reach the lot you are interested in, so use that time to observe how other bidders behave. When it's the turn of your car, attract the auctioneer's attention and make an early bid. The auctioneer will then look to you for a reaction every time another bid is made. Usually the bids will be in fixed increments until the bidding slows, when smaller increments will often be accepted before the hammer falls. If you want to withdraw

from the bidding, make sure the auctioneer understands your intentions – a vigorous shake of the head when he or she looks to you for the next bid should do the trick. Assuming that you are the successful bidder, the auctioneer will note your card or paddle number, and from that moment on you will be responsible for the vehicle. If a car you like is unsold, either because it failed to reach the reserve or because there was little interest, it may be possible to negotiate with the owner, via the auctioneers, after the sale is over.

Successful bid
There are two more items to think about. How to get the car home, and insurance. If you can't drive the car, your own or a hired trailer is one option, and another is to have the vehicle shipped using the facilities of a local company. The auction house will have details of companies specialising in the transport of cars.

Insurance for immediate cover can usually be purchased on site, but it may be more cost-effective to make arrangements with your own insurance company in advance, and then call to confirm the full details.

eBay and other online auctions
eBay and other online auctions could land you a car at a bargain price, though you'd be foolhardy to bid without examining the car first, something most vendors

Auctions are a quick and easy way of disposing of surplus cars, but also of offloading dodgy and knackered ones, although the title at least should be clear, and you can examine them quite closely and hear the engine running.

encourage. A useful feature of eBay is that the geographical location of the car is shown, so you can narrow your choices to those within a realistic radius of home. Be prepared to be outbid in the last few moments of the auction: there is software designed to achieve just that. Remember, your bid is binding and that it will be very, very difficult to get restitution in the case of a crooked vendor fleecing you – caveat emptor.

Be aware that some cars offered for sale in online auctions are 'ghost' cars. Don't part with any cash without being sure that the vehicle does actually exist and is as described: pre-bidding inspection is a must

Auctioneers
Barrett-Jackson
www.barrett-jackson.com
Bonhams www.bonhams.com
British Car Auctions (BCA)
www.bca-europe.com or
www.british-car-auctions.co.uk
Cheffins www.cheffins.co.uk

Christies www.christies.com
Coys www.coys.co.uk
eBay www.eBay.com
H&H www.classic-auctions.co.uk
RM www.rmauctions.com
Shannons www.shannons.com.au
Silver www.silverauctions.com

11 Paperwork
– correct documentation is essential!

Classic, collector, and prestige cars usually come with a large portfolio of paperwork accumulated and passed on by a succession of proud owners. This documentation represents the history of the car, and from it can be deduced the level of care the car has received, and how much it's been used. All this information will be priceless to you as the new owner, so be wary of cars with little paperwork to support their claimed history, unless they're too old and cheap for previous owners to have bothered keeping records.

Correct registration

My first kit car was a Triumph Midge, built in about 1985. It used a 2-litre 1971 Triumph Vitesse for a donor, and had a new chassis. It was inspected at my home by an official who said it was very nice, and gave me a new chassis number. The car is now a tax-free 1971 Triumph Midge, and until recently needed an annual MOT. Easy.

The ID plates on old British cars are easily transferable to another, and it might well have been easier to change a body tub or a chassis for a better one than to repair it. If the repaired Triumph that was fitted with another better body already had a registration, tax and MOT you would be tempted just to move the old identity over. After all, what's the difference?

Legally, the new shells supplied by British Motor Heritage for Minis, MGs and Triumph TR6s are regarded as repair panels, and the 'repaired' re-shelled vehicle retains its original identity.

Using a secondhand replacement body of the same type that may or may not have come with an identity should cause no bother, as long as you have proof of purchase, and/or the old ID paperwork. Changing a saloon to a convertible would invite questions, but the answer is that the different tops bolt on and are interchangeable. If identity machinations come to light later, you might end up in a world of clerical pain. It's not a common problem at all, but check that the VIN plates look original. There's no chassis number stamped on the Herald or Vitesse chassis, just a commission number on the body.

The author's Triumph Midge. Kit cars are very cheap due to ill-informed prejudice. This is Vitesse-based, weighs about 1700lb even with a very strong kit chassis, looks like 1935 and is indecently rapid. What's not to like?

The lack of future MOT requirement will let some ringers and stolen cars continue to be bought and sold, so taking a prospective purchase for an MOT to put it through the computer system before buying it is an even smarter move now than it used to be.

Registration documents

All countries/states have some form of registration for private vehicles, whether it's like the American 'pink slip' system or the British 'registration document' system.

It is essential to check that the registration document is genuine, that it relates to the car in question, and that all the vehicle's details are correctly recorded, including commission/VIN and engine numbers (if these are shown). If you are buying from the previous owner, their name and address will be recorded in the document: this will not be the case if you are buying from a dealer. In the UK the current (Euro-aligned) registration document is named 'V5C,' and is printed in coloured sections of blue, green and pink. The blue section relates to the car specification, the green section has details of the new owner and the pink section is sent to the DVLA in the UK when the car is sold. A small section in yellow deals with selling the car within the motor trade. Due to the introduction of important new legislation on data protection, it is no longer possible to acquire, from the British DVLA, a list of previous owners of a car you own, or are intending to purchase. This scenario will also apply to dealerships and other specialists, from who you may wish to make contact and acquire information on previous ownership and work carried out.

Monocoques and IVA

The less fortunate classic car owners whose cars have monocoque construction are not allowed to alter the monocoques in any way, unless they submit them for an expensive government test. This applies even if they have just altered a Mini dashboard panel to fit a Weber air filter.

Heralds and Vitesses have a separate chassis, so you can feel free to alter the bodywork as much as you like without government interference. Another small advantage to the Triumph lifestyle.

Roadworthiness certificate

Most country/state administrations require that vehicles are regularly tested to prove that they are safe to use on the public highway and do not produce excessive emissions. In the UK that test (the MOT) is carried out at approved testing stations, for a fee. It is no longer applied to Heralds or Vitesses because of their age, which is a mixed blessing. In the USA the requirement varies, but most states insist on an emissions test every two years as a minimum, while the police are charged with pulling over unsafe-looking vehicles.

Changed legislation in the UK means that the seller of a car must surrender any existing road fund licence, and it is the responsibility of the new owner to re-tax the vehicle at the time of purchase and before the car can be driven on the road. It's therefore vital to see the Vehicle Registration Certificate (V5C) at the time of purchase, and to have access to the New Keeper Supplement (V5C/2), allowing the buyer to obtain road tax immediately.

If the car is untaxed because it has not been used for a period of time, the owner has to inform the licensing authorities, otherwise the vehicle's date-related registration number will be lost and there will be a painful amount of paperwork to get it re-registered.

Road licence

The administration of every country/state charges some kind of tax for the use of its road system. UK classic cars older than 40 years, including the Herald and Vitesse, are exempt from paying road tax, but owners must still file the annual application paperwork or face a fine. The actual form of the 'road licence' and how it is displayed varies widely from country to country and state to state.

Whatever the form of the road licence, it must relate to the vehicle carrying it and must be present and valid if the car is to be driven on the public highway legally. The value of the licence will depend on the length of time it remains valid. In the UK if a car is untaxed because it has not been used for a period of time, the owner has to inform the licencing authorities, otherwise the vehicle's date-related registration number will be lost and there will be a painful amount of paperwork to get it re-registered, and potential tax fines as well. In the UK a car not on the road must be recorded as being off the road with a SORN certificate. If you buy a car it must be taxed or SORNed immediately. UK government fines start from ●x80 and rise to ●x1000 plus potential clamping and having your vehicle crushed or sold if you do not comply. They are the Borg. Resistance is futile.

Service history

Often these cars will have been serviced at home by enthusiastic (and hopefully capable) owners. Nevertheless, try to obtain as many receipts and other paperwork pertaining to the car as you can. Items such as the original bill of sale, build manual, parts invoices, and repair bills add great deal to the story and the character of the car. A sales brochure is a useful document and something that you could well have to search hard to locate in future years.

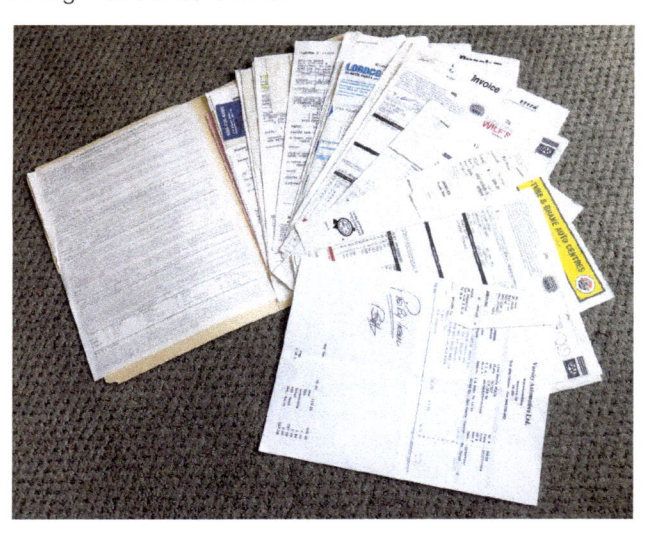

If the seller claims to have carried out regular servicing, ask what work was completed and when, and seek some evidence of it being carried out. Your assessment of the car's overall condition should tell you whether the seller's claims are genuine.

For a home-serviced car, ask if the front suspension trunnions (the pins on which the front wheels swivel) have been regularly greased. The correct answer should be "No, they use oil." As the trunnions can snap and lose a wheel, they need the right lubrication.

12 What's it worth?
– let your head rule your heart

These are the badges we're looking for on the back of the Vitesse. 2-litre is 105bhp and the overdrive means relaxed cruising. The 1.6 Vitesse 6 is sweeter and revvier, if the soundtrack is important, and the choice of soft or hard roof is yours to make.

Condition and model
It's up to you to decide how pristine a car you want, and how much it's worth to you. A top low-miles sales-red overdrive Vitesse is still only in the ten grand arena, which is very good value when you put it up against any of the half-million remaining baggy old Porsche 911s, overvalued at three times that by fashion-conscious brand junkies. That Vitesse valuation will change upwards as time goes on.

If you don't fancy the more ambitious six-cylinder engine in a pretty little classic car, the price you need to pay depends on how much hassle/entertainment you want. All old Triumphs need regular monitoring of fluid levels and issues arising, and regular servicing. Nissan Micras they are not.

A Triumph in sound condition bought for a highish price, well maintained, should give little future mechanical trouble, and none of it will be very expensive.

If you like getting hands-on and Saturday pottering, you can buy a car in poorer

72

condition for very little money, and improve it as you go. Triumphs are simple and accessible, with few complications, and they can be fettled with Halfords tools.

The early cars from the 1960s will continue to rise in value, and they are visibly classic with old-style lights and sharp period Michelotti styling. The dashboards and interiors are also very 1960s. Repairs and restorations are basically the same price for all small Triumphs. The 1300 is the favourite engine among the cognoscenti: it revs freely and makes a nice noise.

The later 13/60 Heralds were updated with a two-headlight bonnet similar to the four-headlight Vitesse bonnet in shape, but less aggressively styled.

The result was still very attractive, but people prefer classic cars to look more classic, so the earlier cars may progressively be worth more.

The value ratio is currently Vitesse at the top, followed by 12/50, then to some extent 13/60. This ratio between the models will stay similar as values rise.

Unless you have a fixed idea of the period of car you want, concentrating on finding a really good Triumph at the right price with some flexibility over the year will offer the best options.

Gentry is a Herald-based replica of a 1950s MG sports car, and is now a classic in its own right. An attractive, solid, well-made car using the Herald/Vitesse chassis and mechanicals. (Courtesy Rob Hawkins)

Desirable options/extras

Overdrive is a very pleasing option, improving cabin noise, engine life and fuel economy with a 20 per cent reduction in cruising rpm. A non-functional overdrive is quite likely to have a minor electrical or earthing issue.

Works steel hardtops as fitted to Spitfires are not an option for the Herald family, although the saloon roof does just unbolt and come off.

Honeybourne Mouldings makes a light detachable fibreglass hardtop for Vitesse and Herald convertibles. Hardtops reduce noise, draughts, vandalism and theft, and come off quite quickly for fine winter days.

A rare genuine Herald Coupé steel roof would be a bonus, but finding one of those not already attached to a valuable Coupé is unlikely.

Undesirable features

Among the Herald and Vitesse models there aren't really any specific undesirable features other than a shared propensity to rust, and dodgy rear suspension. Very early Heralds have a dashboard made out of porridge rather than veneered wood, but the value of a good early car would preclude the permanent retro-fitting of a better-looking dash.

Striking a deal

Negotiate on the basis of your condition assessment, your estimate of the actual mileage, and the cost of having things re-done your way. Judge how badly the owner needs the money.

Be firm about your estimate of a car's real value, but don't be completely intractable: a small compromise on the part of the seller or buyer will often achieve a deal.

Around Christmas has proven to be the best time of year to buy a convertible car.

Triumph-based Gentry kit car interior is a work of art. Let's just keep quiet about the benefits of kit cars, buy a good one for peanuts, and forget about body rust forever. (Courtesy Rob Hawkins)

13 Do you really want to restore?
– it'll take longer and cost more than you think

If you have reasonable mechanical skills and patience but are restricted by a small budget, you can do very well by taking advantage of somebody else's misfortune and buying an abandoned project. There is a dangerous 90 per cent-completed stage in any car project when people simply get fed up with the whole thing. Wives get sick of being abandoned for a year's worth of evenings. Recession, redundancy, and children show up. 🟡x12,000 worth of hoarded parts and a mostly-finished car can be bought for a small percentage of that amount.

A mid-budget MIG welder is fine for home body restoration. The cheapest ones like this don't help the learning process, although they still do the job. MIG welding is genuinely an accessible art.

You have to be able to assemble things, glue things, adjust things, lift things, and scramble around and under things in order to build a car, but if you can achieve successful and tidy household DIY you can probably succeed in completing a Triumph restoration. There is much satisfaction in doing so.

Triumphs are actually rather good targets for restoration as they come completely to pieces in a few manageable lumps. In the UK, space tends to be at a premium, and Heralds and Vitesses can be stripped into three large pieces – front, body tub, and chassis. Each can then be manoeuvred around, upended for access, and welded where needed, with the refurbished rolling chassis covered up and used as a table to present the other large parts at a usefully accessible height for whatever attention they need.

This is what your first welding attempts will look like. Keep at it, though – improvement in your skills will be quite quick after an hour of practice.

Dynamat noise reduction represents new technology that can be usefully applied to old cars.

Welding with MIG welders is actually quite accessible for novices, with the recommendation that you buy a mid-range budget MIG welder: really cheap ones contribute inadequacy problems to your lack-of-skill, but paying a bit more for a mid-range hobby welder makes learning to weld easier.

The revealed nastiness and huge task list of a major-project Triumph will be daunting, so avoid looking at the whole thing – fix the floors, then the sills, then the other little welding bits, and the tub is done. Next, pick another task and focus on that.

Make arrangements to prevent divorce. The hundreds of happy hours of solo garage pottering is time not spent with your loved ones. That may have consequences: budget for kitchen refits, new sofas, and pretending to enjoy family holidays.

Potential problems include unexpected setbacks such as rebuilt but unused hydraulic cylinders rusting in damp garage storage, and previously restored components having to be restored again. There is also the statistical inevitability that some abandoned restorations were started by idiots. You may have to take the car completely apart and start again; not necessarily a bad thing.

You can incorporate modern technology with electronic ignition, which is usefully immune to distributor shaft wear. Doesn't work for me; does work for most people.

I have had a 100 per cent failure rate with aftermarket electronic ignition, so I keep the original distributor in a bag in the boot.

When eventually fitting unleaded exhaust valve seats in a well-used Triumph, you might as well polish the ports and match them to the exhaust manifold bore as well, for extra smoothness and a few more bhp.

Drilling out the valve seats is a professional machining job, but smoothing the port walls is well within the amateur purview.

Another upgrade that can either effectively provide or replace an overdrive unit is the five-speed gearbox conversion: Frontline Developments supplies this one.

Many Triumphisti will suggest replacing Strombergs with SU carbs. Don't. A Stromberg with a new diaphragm is more efficient.

79

14 Paint problems
– bad complexion, including dimples, pimples and bubbles

Paint faults are generally due to poor paint preparation: the prep is 90 per cent of a good finish. Some of the following issues will appear as you paint a car, some can be used to knock the price down before you buy one.

It is still possible to spray-paint a car at home with a small compressor and a gun, although you ideally need to track down oil-based paint to achieve toughness and gloss.

Caution! Don't attempt a two-pack isocyanate paint finish at home – it contains cyanide and is as dangerous as you think.

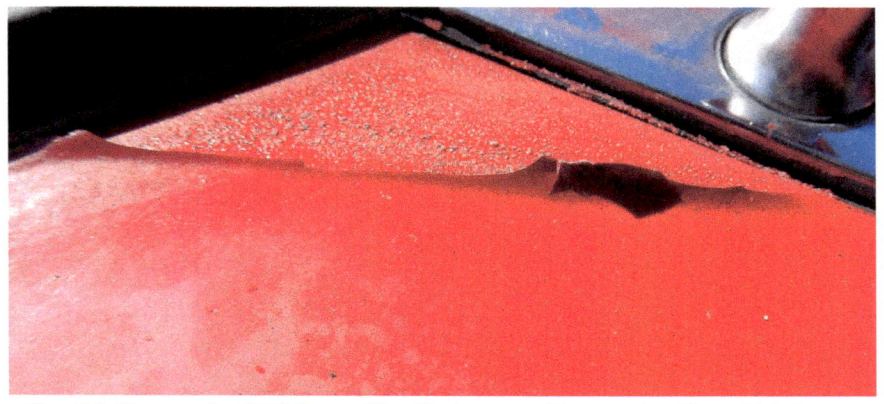

Possibly the worst paint job ever. Very bad prep and too much paint, which is now flaking off in chunks. It will need to be stripped to bare metal and done properly. But the car in question is unsaleable so you *could* snag it for a brutally low offer.

Fading
Polishing cars is not just a way to avoid daytime television: it provides the paint with a layer of protection. When the polish layer has faded, the paint itself is exposed, and it begins to oxidise and go flat and dull. Cutting back the outer layer of paint with mildly abrasive compounds such as T-Cut can sometimes bring the finish back to life, but only a limited number of times, as you're taking off a layer of the paint each time you do it.

Orange peel
This appears as an uneven paint surface, and looks like the tiny dimples

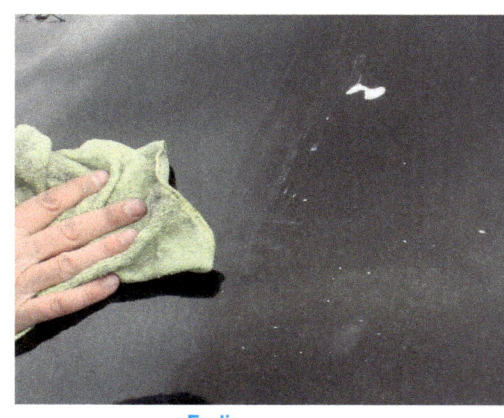

Fading.

on orange skins. It's caused by the failure of atomized paint droplets to blend when they hit the surface. If the paint's thick enough, you can sometimes rub orange peel down to a good finish with rubbing compound or extremely fine grades of wet and dry paper used with plenty of water. Knock the cost of a repaint off your offer anyway.

Cracking and crazing

This is cracking, fine crazing or a 'crackle' effect resembling an old-school MGB dashboard. Severe cases are probably caused by too much paint, or too much filler beneath the paint. Inadequate paint-stirring is another possible cause, as is a chemical reaction with previous layers of paint. Back down to the primer coat and start again, I'm afraid.

Blistering

Usually caused by chemical reactions beneath the paint. Has to be taken back to primer or bare metal, and an additional isolating primer should be applied before the respray.

Orange peel.

Crazing.

This paint is very thick, but so poorly executed that it can be prised off with a penknife blade. The only solution is a bare-metal respray.

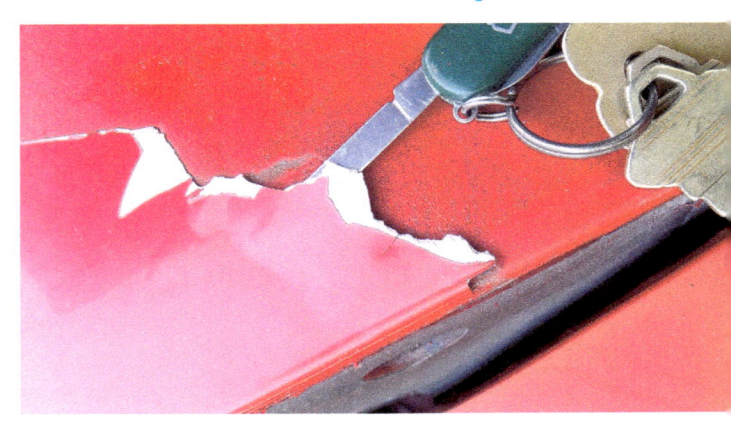

Micro-blistering
Usually the result of an amateur or backyard respray where inadequate heating has allowed moisture to settle on the car before, during or after spraying. Consult a paint specialist, but usually damaged paint will have to be removed before a partial or full respray. Micro-blistering can also be caused on existing paint by using cheap car covers that don't 'breathe.' Cheap tarpaulins can also leach chemicals into paint, as I found out to my cost.

Micro-blistering.

Peeling
Often a problem with metallic and two-pack paintwork, when the sealing clearcoat laquer becomes damaged and begins to peel off. Poorly applied paint may also peel. The remedy is to strip it off and start again. You don't necessarily need to take it back to bare metal, as the existing primer and base colour coats are a good base for new paint, particularly if it's the same colour.

Dimples or Fisheyes
Dimples in paintwork are frequently caused by residues of polish (particularly silicone types) not being removed properly before painting. Paint removal and repainting is the only solution.

Base and clearcoat paint jobs are fine if the clearcoat continues to stick to the base coat. Good prep and good materials are key, but were apparently not applied in this case. Heralds and Vitesses don't have metallic paint, which is a bonus.

15 Problems due to lack of use
– just like their owners, small Triumphs need exercise!

Cars, like humans, work better if exercised regularly. Driving a classic car at least ten miles, once a week, is recommended. It's also good for your soul.

Barn finds sound intriguing, and certainly dragging a dusty treasure into the sunlight after decades of slumber is romantic and rather magical. The recent deeply silly auction prices paid for barn find wreckage reflect that. However, even if rust has been avoided by long, dry storage, other issues are lining up to cause problems. Buying cars that have been in regular use is a much better idea.

The fuel tank may look reasonably solid from the outside, but we don't know what nastiness lurks within. Clean it out and potentially save a lot of grief in the future.

Seized components

Pistons in brake callipers, master and slave cylinders can seize. Clutches may seize if the plate sticks to the flywheel because of corrosion, although once freed they're usually fine. The gearbox may need to be removed to rectify this if the plate is properly stuck to the flywheel face. A big screwdriver can sometimes be poked in between the clutch plate and flywheel to break the stiction. Handbrakes (parking brakes) can seize if the cables and linkages rust, or if the rear brake linings stick to the drums. Drums hit too hard can both dent and shatter, which is rather unfair. Pistons can seize in engine cylinder bores due to corrosion, and valves can stick in their seats. A stuck engine can sometimes be freed with releasing agent, light oil down the bores, and gentle tapping.

Fluids
Old, acidic oil can corrode bearings, and also deposits icky kak (a technical term) in the sump and oil galleries. Don't use flushing oil as it can flush hard particles into the bearings. Old or uninhibited coolant can corrode internal waterways, particularly in aluminium engines. Lack of antifreeze in coolant can cause core (freeze) plugs to be pushed out, and can even crack blocks or heads. Silt settling and solidifying in radiator tubes and blocking water passages, often at the back of engines where coolant flow is slow and particles drop out of suspension, can cause overheating. Brake fluid absorbs water from the atmosphere and should ideally be renewed every two years. Old brake fluid with a high water content causes the pistons in callipers and wheel cylinders to rust and seize, and can also cause brake failure when it boils during hard braking. Fuel tanks usually have some water in them as well as ancient kak from evaporated old fuel. They suffer from rust flakes and particles that clog filters and carbs. They need to be cleaned out and/or repaired after any time out of regular use. Any residual fuel fumes retained make old and nearly empty fuel tanks very effective bombs.

Tyre problems
Tyres that have had the weight of the car on them in a single position for some time will develop flat spots, resulting in some (usually temporary) vibration. Old tyre walls may have cracks or blister-type bulges, meaning new tyres are needed. All tyres should really be replaced after six or seven years.

Shock absorbers (dampers)
With lack of use, the exposed central shafts can rust, then rip up the seals when next used.

Rubber and plastic
Radiator hoses harden, perish and split, resulting in potential total coolant loss. Gaiters/boots can crack. Wiper blades harden in much the same way as tyres.

Electrics
Old cars have earthing or grounding issues at the best of times, as rust insulates rather than conducts electricity. Damp corrodes electrical connections, but cleaning and electrical grease help.
    Batteries left flat for months will die: trickle chargers or solar chargers can prevent this, and the new generation of pulse chargers can sometime revive dead batteries. Wiring insulation can harden and fail, as can the copper strands within the wires.

Exhaust systems
Exhaust gas contains water and corrosive compounds, so exhaust systems can corrode from the inside when the car is not used.

16 The Community
– key people, organisations and companies in the Triumph world

The Triumph Sports Six Club is an excellent introduction to the UK Triumph scene (www.tssc.org.uk). You can either join the forum free by entering a name and password, or you can join the club properly, pay your £44 UK/ £50 worldwide dues and get the club magazine sent. In the free forums you'll find some revealing chat, most of it constructive. The club has marque registers for the different sorts of Triumph, and special tools that can be rented or borrowed. There are area meetings full of people with useful skills and chummy prices on spares. In turn you will find yourself helping to hunt down Triumphs for future new members and trading back and forth with your own stash of spares. Beer, tea, support, and camaraderie are all involved.

CarClubsWorldwide lists 25 Triumph clubs worldwide, so there is definitely one within reach wherever you are. It's always worth joining your local club as there will be somebody who can weld, somebody who can disentangle underdash tagliatelle and make lights work, somebody who can excommunicate evil spirits, and lots of others who can be relied upon to drink your beer and idle around in your garage, supervising and offering useful and amusing comments and suggestions. It's not good clean fun, but it is good fun.

Going to Le Mans, or anywhere else for that matter, in a Triumph with a crowd of other Triumph drivers is thoroughly recommended. I used to organise a Le Mans camping trip for *Kitcar* magazine, which was excellent fun and attracted a good

Triumphs are still a common and popular car, with a healthy club scene and many social opportunities. Shows can be good fun and a well-sorted car will be admired.

crowd: there are many Le Mans trips you can join. Classic Le Mans is probably more suitable for Triumph enthusiasts, although the main Le Mans race must be attended once for bucket list reasons. It just needs to be done, doesn't it?

Trackday action is also strongly recommended, partly because it's enormous fun and partly for safety reasons: if you've pushed your car hard enough to spin it or nearly spin it a few times on the track, you'll know when you're near the limit on the road as well. Don't casually spin off the track, though: if a wheel digs into the grass, you'll roll the car. That is a particularly bad idea in a convertible with no roll over bar.

An insider tip is not to rush to get to a track day early, though – the queue to get on the track will thin out dramatically after lunch as everybody else gets tired and some of their cars break. Also, take spare brake pads: if you're giving your car any real exercise you'll get through a set in a day. Re-tighten your wheel nuts periodically during the day, as they work loose on the track. If you drive an earlier Herald or Vitesse, consider doing something about the rear suspension before you take it out on a track.

The Old English Car Club of British Colombia is a broad church that organises an annual run celebrating the London-Brighton veteran-car run. All Brit cars are welcome, and it's a nice finale to the classic car year. Here, I'm following three Triumphs.

Classic rallies of the lighter sort are excellent, particularly if they're held in France or Belgium. TR3s and TR4s are a more usual classic rallying tool, but a Herald or Vitesse will be eligible for most informal events and some serious Time/Speed/Distance rallies. Be aware, though, that these are also known as divorce rallies.

Scenic and Continental Car Tours is a company that has evolved out of an earlier company that ran excellent Belgian non-competitive weekend rallies: the boss knew Rudy the local police chief who would attend the post-rally banquet, so it was happy bunnies all round.

The classic car show scene is good fun too – there is normally camping during show weekends, and the cheerful company of plenty of other enthusiasts.

The classic car magazines are full of ads for all the shows, and there's usually an autojumble and some useful traders. **Inside tip** – nobody wants to take stuff home again, so prices take a violent dip at the end of the day as traders begin to pack up their tables.

The period picnic set and Bush radio are show props here, but they also do their jobs for real: cricket still features on Radio 4, and Waitrose means picnics are no longer the compulsory cheese sandwiches on white. (Courtesy Keith Evans)

Triumph Car Clubs

Clubs, personnel and contacts change, so nowadays Google is the way to find and join your local Triumph club. General multi-marque classic car clubs are also worth a look: my local Old English Car Club in BC is big, active and enthusiastic, and complements membership of the BC Triumph Registry.

www.practicalclassics.co.uk carries a good and updated car club guide, and googling Triumph Car Club plus your location gets useful results. It also carries regularly updated price trends for each marque.

Paul Barlow's immaculate Vitesse is coming out for the London-Brighton celebration run in Vancouver. I'm beginning to regret not buying that car when I had the chance.

17 Vital statistics
– essential data at your fingertips

Production numbers
Herald Coupé	1959-1964	20,476
Herald 948 and S	1959-1964	94,514
Herald 1200 saloon	1961-1970	201,142
Herald 1200 convertible	1961-1967	43,295
Herald 1200 estate	1961-1967	39,819
Herald 12/50	1963-1967	53,267
Herald 13/60 saloon	1967-1970	40,433
Herald 13/60 estate	1967-1971	11,172
Herald 13/60 convertible	1967-1971	15,467
Courier van	1962-1966	5136
Vitesse 6 saloon	1962-1966	22,814
Vitesse 6 convertible	1962-1966	8447
Vitesse 2-litre saloon	1966-1968	7328
Vitesse 2-litre convertible	1968-1971	3502
Vitesse 2-litre MkII saloon	1968-1971	5649
Vitesse 2-litre MkII convertible	1968-1971	3472
Bond Equipe four-cylinder	1963-1970	2948
Bond Equipe six-cylinder	1967-1970	1430

Compared to the chromed plastic tat that decorates even expensive cars made in 2020, the enamelled chrome-plated badge-work on a period Triumph is entirely pleasing.

Upgrades at a glance
Herald 1200   more power, wooden dashboard, optional twin SU carbs
Herald 12/50   more power, Webasto sliding fabric sunroof, disc brakes
Herald 13/60   more power, restyled interior, new flip front resembling Vitesse
Vitesse 2-litre more power, improved rear suspension

Engines

Herald	948cc OHV straight-four	34.5bhp
Herald 1200	1147cc OHV straight-four	39bhp, later 48bhp
Herald 12/50	1147cc OHV straight-four	51bhp
Herald 13/60	1296cc OHV straight-four	61bhp
Courier van	1147cc OHV straight-four	39bhp, later 48bhp
Vitesse 6	OHV straight-six	70bhp
Vitesse 2-litre	OHV straight-six	104bhp

Transmission/drivetrain
Synchromesh on 2nd, 3rd, top
Vitesse gets optional overdrive on 3rd and 4th from 1964
Vitesse 2-litre uses stronger all-synchro gearbox shared with GT6
Vitesse 2-litre MkII gets improved rear suspension and Rotoflex drive couplings with new lower rear wishbone

Brake system specifications
Drums until about 1967, disc brakes optional from 1962: then disc front, drum rear throughout. Larger discs/drums on Vitesse.

Dimensions

Length	153in (3886mm)
Width	60in (1524mm)
Height	52in (1321mm)
Wheelbase	91in (2311mm)

Heralds and Vitesses are the same length and width.

Weights

Herald 1200 convertible	1598lb (725kg)
Herald 12/50 saloon	1854lb (841kg)
Herald 13/60 estate	1907lb (865kg)
Vitesse saloon	2044lb (927kg)

Performance

Acceleration 0-60mph
Slowest: Herald 948	29.9 seconds
Fastest: Vitesse 2-litre MkII	11.4 seconds

Top speed
Slowest: Herald 948	71mph
Fastest: Vitesse 2-litre MkII	106mph

The Essential Buyer's Guide
ALFASUD
ALFETTA
GT COUPE
SPIDER
TT
TT
BIG HEALEYS
E30 3 SERIES
X5
Z3 ROADSTER
Z4
2CV
DS & ID
REPLICAS
CORVETTE
240Z
DMC-12
124 SPIDER & AZURRA SPIDER
500 & 600
CAPRI
ESCORT
FOCUS MK1 RS & ST170
MODEL A
MODEL T
MUSTANG
MUSTANG
RS Cosworth Sierra & Escort
IMP
E-TYPE
E-type
MARK 1 & 2
NEW XK
S-TYPE
X-TYPE
XJ-S
XJ6, XJ8 & XJR
XK 120, 140 & 150
XK8 & XKR
XJ
XJ40
XJ6, XJ12 & SOVEREIGN
DISCOVERY
DISCOVERY
SERIES I, II & IIA
SERIES III
ELAN
EUROPA
Seven Replicas & Caterham 7
MX-5 MIATA
RX-8
230, 250 & 280SL 'PAGODA'
190
280-560SL & SLC
G-WAGEN
S-CLASS
S-CLASS
SL
SLK
W123
W124
MIDGET & SPRITE
TD, TF & TF1500
MGA
MGB & MGB GT

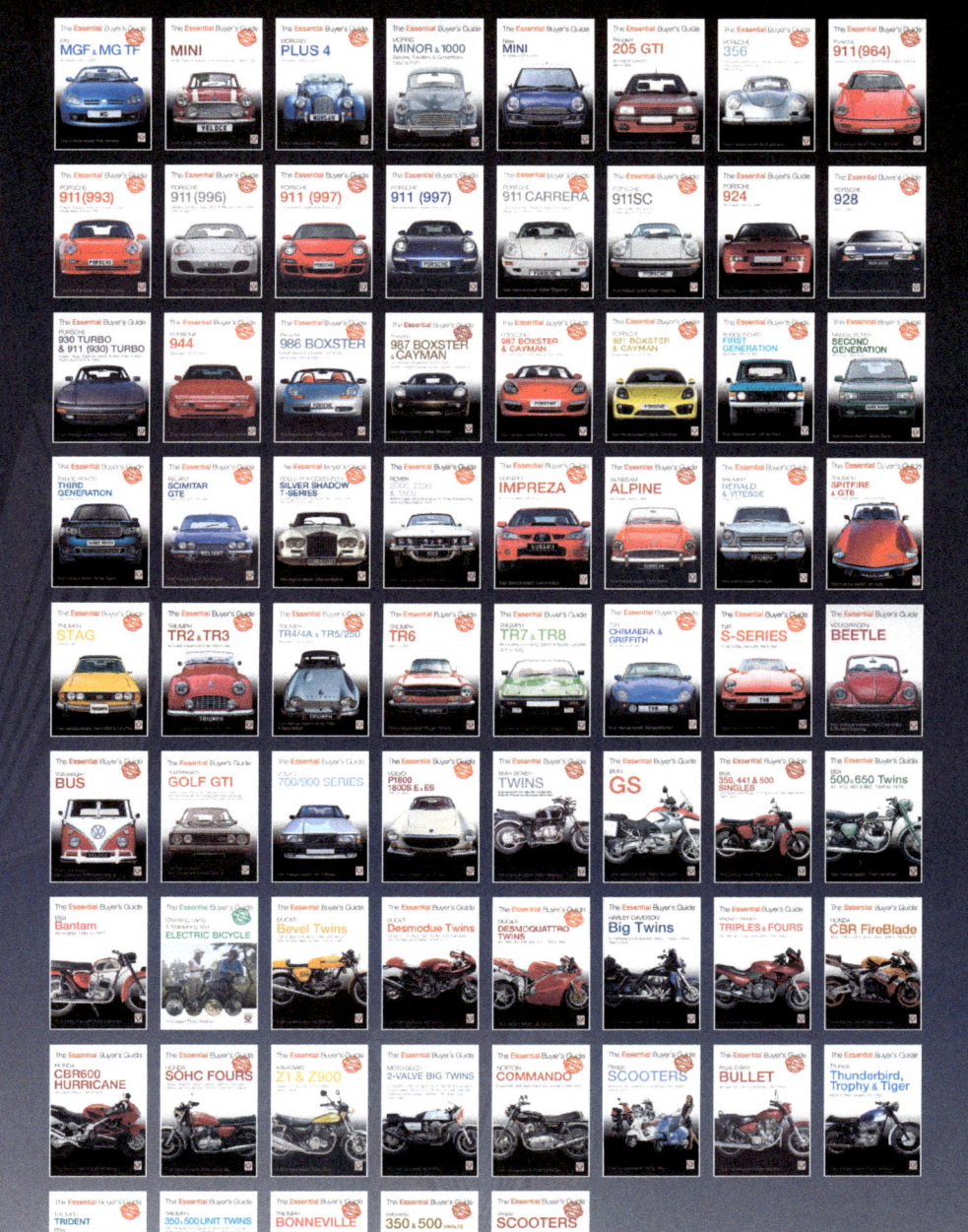

For more details visit: www.veloce.co.uk
email: info@veloce.co.uk
tel: 01305 260068

Triumph Cars
The Complete Story

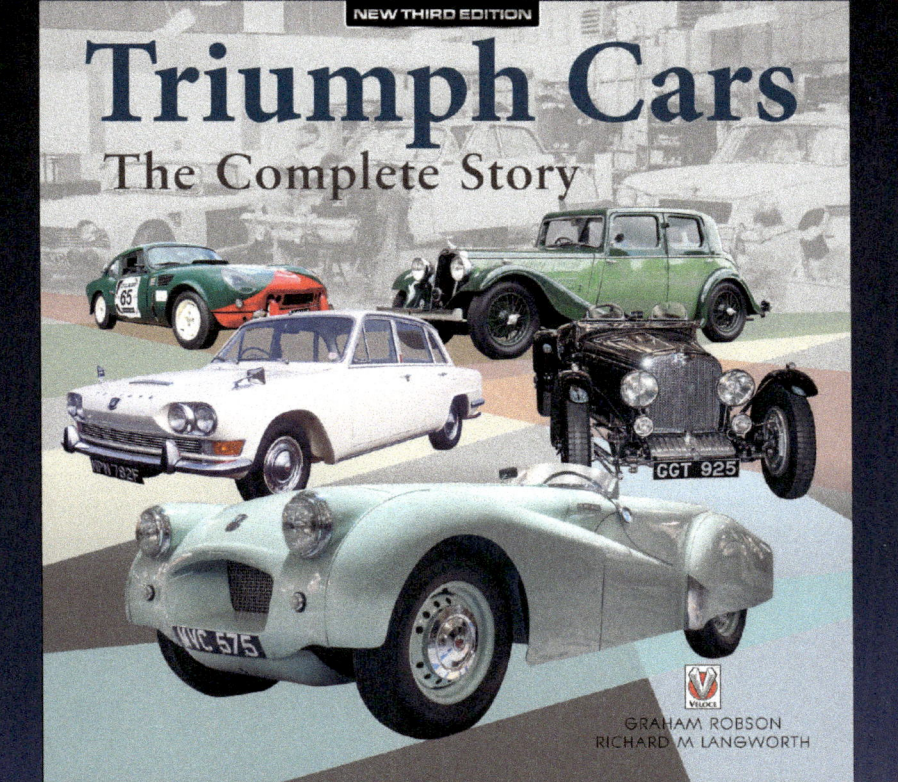

NEW THIRD EDITION

GRAHAM ROBSON
RICHARD M LANGWORTH

Definitive history of the Triumph company from original pedal cycles, to the first Triumph cars, and then every model up to the end of production.

ISBN: 978-1-787112-89-6
Hardback • 25x25cm • 256 pages • 250 pictures

Also from Iain Ayre ...

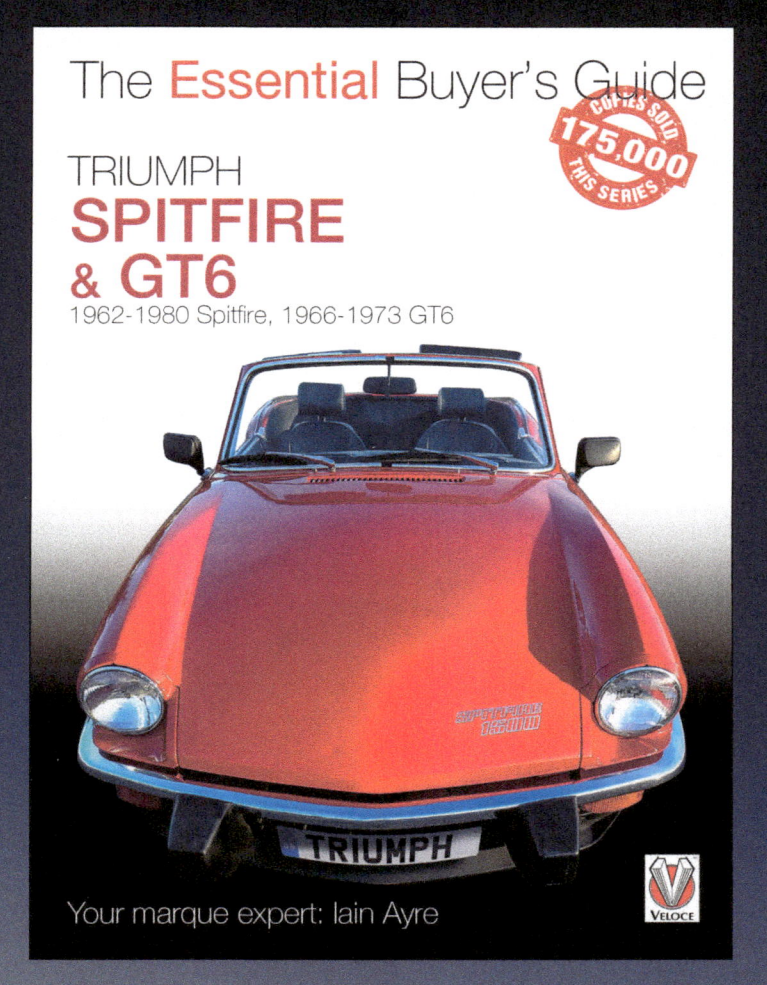

The Essential Buyer's Guide

TRIUMPH
SPITFIRE
& GT6
1962-1980 Spitfire, 1966-1973 GT6

175,000 COPIES SOLD THIS SERIES

Your marque expert: Iain Ayre

ISBN: 978-1-787114-52-4
Paperback • 19.5x13.9cm • 64 pages • 105 pictures

For more information and price details, visit our website at
www.veloce.co.uk • email: info@veloce.co.uk • Tel: +44(0)1305 260068

Index

Amputations, avoidance of 48

Bad points 15, 25
Barn finds 83
Bodywork 52, 48
Bonds 30, 31
Brake fluid issues 84
Brakes 47, 83

Cabin size 9
Club life 85
Compression test 45, 51, 52
Controls 9, 10

Electrics 77, 78

Gearbox, good points 15, 22

History 3-7

Interior 17, 43, 46, 57
Investment 14, 28, 29

Le Mans 85
Luggage 11

Model spec changes 88, 89
MOT tests 56

Oil examination 51
Overdrive 25

Paperwork 27, 41, 49, 69-71
Power 20

Running costs 11, 12

Separate chassis 3, 53, 61-63
Spare parts 12
Steering 9, 10, 47
Suitable oils 19
Suspension 23, 47, 54

Unleaded fuel 51

Welding 75, 76
Wheels and tyres 47, 51, 53, 54

Notes

Notes